THE 100 DAY
ACTION PLAN
TO SAVE
THE PLANET

GE Becker, William S.
180 The 100 day action plan to
.B43 save the planet
2008 751091000439259

NORTH ARKANSAS COLLEGE LIBRARY
1515 Pioneer D:
Harrison, AR 72601

DEMCO

Harrison, AR 72601

ST. MARTIN'S GRIFFIN ⚖ NEW YORK

GE
180
.B43
2008

To my wife, Mary, for the many hours this project has stolen from our life together, and to our children and grandchildren—Aaron, Sarah, Michaelyn, Don, Jason, Megan, and Carter

THE 100 DAY ACTION PLAN TO SAVE THE PLANET. Copyright © 2008 by The Regents of the University of Colorado, a body corporate. All rights reserved. Printed in the United States of America. For information, address St. Martin's Press, 175 Fifth Avenue, New York, N.Y. 10010.

www.stmartins.com

Print ISBN-13: 978-0-312-57541-0
Print ISBN-10: 0-312-57541-6

E-book ISBN-13: 978-1-4299-5357-3
E-book ISBN-10: 1-4299-5357-8

First Edition: November 2008

10   9   8   7   6   5   4   3   2   1

CONTENTS

FOREWORD

The 44th President of the United States will take the oath of office on January 20, 2009. From that moment forward, he will have a relatively short honeymoon period during which he has the best chance of advancing his agenda. This book is an action plan for the new President to attack the problem of global climate change during his first 100 days in office.

Every president over the last thirty years has known about climate change. It is the most dangerous and difficult challenge of our time, and it remains largely unaddressed. While scientific research has reached a consensus that human activity already is causing worldwide climate change, America has lacked the political will to do something about it. Since the oil embargoes of the 1970s, every president has gone on record in support of reducing America's dependence on foreign oil, a necessary step for both energy and climate security; presidents as far back as Lyndon Johnson have been advised about the dangers of climate change. But today, the United States imports more oil and emits more greenhouse gases than ever before.

In 2007, the Intergovernmental Panel on Climate Change (IPCC)—the largest international science collaboration in history—concluded unequivocally that climate change is underway, that it is primarily the result of our consumption of fossil fuels, and that time is growing short if we are to avoid catastrophic consequences on a global scale. "What we do in the next two to three years will determine our future," says Rajendra Pachauri, the head of the

IPCC. "This is the defining moment." It has been left to the new President to define how the United States will respond.

By focusing on the first 100 days, this book underscores the need for urgent action. America's greenhouse gas emissions are growing by 1.5 percent each year. The IPCC has concluded that worldwide greenhouse gas emissions must be stabilized and begin to decline by 2015, just six years after the next President takes the oath of office.

A 100-day action plan carries symbolic weight, too. President Franklin Roosevelt, whose leadership during two critical national crises is often used as a model for what must happen now, framed his own 100-day plan for the period between the opening and closing of the 73rd Congress in 1933. During that time, according to historian Arthur Schlesinger Jr., Roosevelt "sent fifteen messages to Congress, guided fifteen major laws to enactment, delivered ten speeches, held press conferences and cabinet meetings twice a week, conducted talks with foreign heads of state, sponsored an international conference, made all the major decisions in domestic and foreign policy, and never displayed fright or panic and rarely even bad temper."

It's an inspiring example, but we are now facing a different sort of crisis. The crises that FDR faced during his presidency were clearly visible and obvious: the Great Depression and World War II. The climate crisis is far more insidious; vested interests continue to sow doubt that it is real; and the solution will require a literal transformation of the industrial world's economies.

The recommendations in these pages are the result of a two-year effort by the Presidential Climate Action Project at the University of Colorado Denver. I'm often asked how it got started. The short answer is that the project is the brainchild of Dr. David Orr, the noted environmental educator and author at Oberlin College.

The long answer goes back to the 2004 presidential election. At the time, I was beginning my twelfth year as an official at the U.S. Department of Energy. Like many of my colleagues, I had spent my career pushing the United States to begin the transition to a new energy economy powered by renewable resources. When George W. Bush was elected to a second term that year, I was at first shocked, then depressed, that the American people had decided to retain a White House that would be a wholly owned subsidiary of the oil, gas, and coal industries for another four crucial years. I decided I had to make a choice. I either would move to another country so that my taxes would no longer support Bush's policies, or I would try to "light a candle."

I decided on the candle. I resolved to pull together many of America's foremost experts on green energy, climate change, and sustainable development and create a "Sustainable America" action agenda in time to give it to whoever was elected to the presidency in 2008. My starting point was the work of the President's Council on Sustainable Development (PCSD), which was convened by the Clinton administration. From 1993 to 1999, the PCSD developed more than 140 recommendations for policies and initiatives that would make the United States more sustainable, but its body of thoughtful ideas was ignored when the Bush administration took office.

The first step was to recruit the two co-chairs of the PCSD—Ray Anderson and Jonathan Lash—to lead an advisory committee that would guide the project. Ray, the founder and chairman of the board of one of the greenest companies on the planet—Interface Inc. in Atlanta—agreed immediately. He helped me recruit Jonathan, head of the World Resources Institute, to be co-chair.

We devised a plan to hold four National Leadership Summits

for a Sustainable America during 2006 and 2007. The Johnson Foundation offered us the use of their Wingspread Conference Center in Wisconsin for all four meetings.

While the objective of the conferences·was to write an action plan on sustainable development, it quickly became apparent during the first summit in June 2006 that we could not discuss sustainability without tackling climate change. It was, and is, the mother of all sustainability issues. It was at this meeting that David Orr proposed a 100-day plan for presidential leadership.

As a first step, and with the objective of speaking with one voice on climate change, the forty participants produced "The Wingspread Principles on the U.S. Response to Global Warming," and circulated it on the Internet for signatures. These principles became the guideposts for the work to follow.

Later that year, a mutual friend introduced me to Gary Hart, retired U.S. Senator and two-time presidential candidate, now a visiting scholar at the University of Colorado Denver. Hart, one of the nation's most influential new thinkers on national security, immediately saw the importance of climate change. He agreed to join Ray Anderson as co-chair of a Presidential Climate Action Project, or PCAP, as we called it.

I retired from the Department of Energy on January 1, 2007, to begin work on PCAP. We formed a new national advisory committee that now includes Dr. Orr; Dr. D. James Baker, former head of the National Oceanic and Atmospheric Administration; Vice Admiral Richard Truly, a two-time shuttle astronaut and former NASA administrator; Theodore Roosevelt IV, chair of the Pew Center on Global Climate Change; John Petersen, the highly regarded futurist and head of the Arlington Institute; Hunter Lovins, president of Natural Capitalism Solutions; Terry Tamminen, the architect of Governor Arnold Schwarzenegger's pioneering climate policies in

California; Larry Schweiger, head of the National Wildlife Federation; James Gustave "Gus" Speth, dean of Yale's School of Forestry and Environmental Studies; Scott Bernstein of the Center for Neighborhood Technologies; Van Jones, founder of the Green for All movement; and several other distinguished experts.

After eleven months of intensive research, consultation, and writing, we released the preliminary action plan on December 4, 2007. It contained more than three hundred specific proposals for federal policies, programs, executive orders, and legislation across fourteen topic areas—among them climate policy, energy policy, economics, stewardship, state and local adaptation, transportation, and buildings. Among other goals, the three hundred policies were designed to achieve:

- Zero-carbon buildings by 2030
- Dramatic cuts in oil use for transportation
- An economy-wide drive to improve America's energy efficiency
- An 80 to 100 percent reduction in greenhouse gas emissions by midcentury
- An end to federal subsidies of carbon-intensive fuels
- A moratorium on new, conventional coal-fired power plants
- Carbon neutrality for the world's biggest single energy consumer, the U.S. government
- An active and constructive role by the United States in the international effort to control greenhouse gas emissions

Since releasing the first plan, we have continued commissioning research and convening the nation's top environmental, business, science, academic, and policy experts with the goal of providing the President-elect and his transition team an updated action agenda just after the November 4 election.

What we intend to demonstrate—and what I hope to convey in this book—is that global climate change will not be solved with a single bill in Congress, or with the President's bully pulpit, or by hoping the marketplace will work its magic with no help from the federal government. The Presidential Climate Action Plan is based on the idea that an adequate response to this most complex of problems will require every tool in the toolbox—in the White House, the Congress, state and local governments, the business sector, on Main Street, and in households across America.

From the first 100 minutes of his inaugural address through the next 100 days, the next President must put America back on the path to achieving energy and climate security.

The full Presidential Climate Action Plan has been delivered to the President-elect and his transition team, and we hope it provides many good ideas for leadership. You can find the full document at www.climateactionproject.com.

INTRODUCTION

Presidential Power and the 100-Day Plan

As he delivers his inaugural address, the new President will set the tone of his leadership for the next four years. The world community will be listening closely for signs of his—and America's—intentions in regard to energy and climate security.

It's difficult to exaggerate the importance of those signals. The nation's de facto energy policy has been to prolong the carbon economy of the past two hundred years. Climate change has been ignored in the highest places. Every generation faces challenges and every president shapes history, but this moment is special. The work ahead of us will determine the habitability of the planet on which we and future generations live. We who are alive today will lay the foundation for security and prosperity for generations to come, or we will create a world in which security, prosperity, and even liberty are relics of the past. It is a privilege, a challenge, and a profound obligation to be alive today and to be responsible for this historic passage.

The President will have his work cut out for him. To carry out the goals of this 100-day action plan, he will need to use his executive powers as well as the power of persuasion, work with Congress on a comprehensive legislative program, and collaborate with international organizations and other countries working on a global solution to this global problem.

Here are the key parts of the plan. The President should:

- Take early action by using the powers Congress already has delegated to the executive branch
- Move rapidly away from investments that lock the nation into more long-term carbon emissions
- Rebuild the federal government's leadership capacity by restoring respect for science and bringing America's best experts on energy and climate security into public service
- Mobilize the marketplace to build a new twenty-first century economy
- Launch an economy-wide "clean energy surge"
- Ensure that climate action is equitable and fair
- Create an agenda for natural resource stewardship that responds to climate change
- Help the nation adapt to the climate changes already underway
- Redefine national security to include climate and energy security
- Work with leading governors and mayors to create an intergovernmental action plan
- Reengage the community of nations to find solutions to the climate and energy crises
- Work closely with Congress to create additional laws and to fund the programs we need to effectively address energy and climate security

What's at stake is not just America's credibility around the world. As I will explain in the pages that follow, climate action is important to our national security, our economic stability, and to the health, welfare, and quality of life of the American people.

But first, I'd like to set the context by recapping the history of the current climate crisis and reviewing the latest research so the urgency of the solutions outlined here is clear.

1.

What's the Problem?

If you're reading this book, you probably don't need to be convinced that global climate change is real, or that its increasing pace presents the nation with a challenge as profound as any we've faced. But I will take a moment to explain the problem and to recap some of the most significant—and alarming—developments of the past few years.

The global climate that has made the planet hospitable to life as we know it depends upon a balancing act that works roughly like this: When living things die, they emit carbon as they decompose. Some of that carbon enters the atmosphere. The rest is absorbed and stored by plants, the oceans, and soils.

The carbon that enters the atmosphere acts like a blanket of insulation, trapping some of the sun's heat so that the planet remains the right temperature for humans and other species alive today. If too much carbon goes into the atmosphere, the planet gets warmer; too little, and the planet cools.

In effect, the earth breathes, inhaling carbon during warm seasons when plant life grows; exhaling it in cold seasons when plant life goes dormant. Forests and other vegetation are its lungs. This breathing is part of a natural cycle that maintains the carbon balance, not unlike that maintained by us humans as we breathe in oxygen and breathe out carbon dioxide.

One factor that created the friendly carbon balance we know today was that nature stored enormous amounts of carbon underground long ago: once-living plants and animals that over the eons became oil, gas, and coal. That carbon was permanently sequestered in the earth until we began digging it up and burning it on a large scale to fuel the industrial age.

The combustion of these fuels has released their carbon into the atmosphere, in such large quantities that the earth is losing its carbon balance. Carbon dioxide and other greenhouse gases* are increasing the atmosphere's insulating effect and trapping more of the sun's heat. As always, soils, oceans, and plants try to absorb these emissions. But as a result of agricultural practices, the loss of tropical forests, and the natural limitations of carbon sinks, they have not kept up with the intense emissions of the industrial era. The result is an increase in the earth's temperature, a trend that scientists have physically measured.

Another important effect of warming is what scientists call "positive feedback loops"—events that speed up the climate change process. For example, polar ice reflects some of the sun's heat. When it melts, the surfaces of the exposed land or water reflect less heat and absorb more, accelerating global warming.

Today, the concentrations of carbon dioxide in the atmosphere are rapidly approaching the point at which they are "too high to

---

* There are six major greenhouse gases. Carbon dioxide is the heat-trapping gas most often discussed in relation to climate change because it is one of the most common and most persistent. Once in the atmosphere, it remains for thousands of years. Because of that fact, many scientists communicate greenhouse gas reduction goals in terms of carbon dioxide (CO_2) emissions. For ease of communications in this book, I use the terms "carbon dioxide" and "greenhouse gas emissions" interchangeably.

maintain the climate to which humanity, wildlife, and the rest of the biosphere are adapted," according to Dr. James Hansen, chief climate scientist at the National Aeronautics and Space Administration's Goddard Institute for Space Studies. In other words, without rapid action to curb greenhouse gas emissions, the twenty-thousand-year period that has proven so hospitable to life as we know it will be gone, replaced by rising sea levels, dying oceans, severe drought, extreme weather, spreading disease, and species extinction, among other things.

The scientific consensus is that to have a fifty-fifty chance of avoiding the worst consequences of climate change, we must hold global warming to no more than 2 degrees centigrade (3.6 degrees Fahrenheit) above preindustrial levels. That will require that we keep atmospheric concentrations of carbon dioxide at about 450 parts per million or less. They already are at 385 parts per million and climbing. Hansen believes concentrations must be much lower, eventually returning to 300–350 parts per million.

While a 2-degree centigrade temperature increase doesn't seem like much of a difference, it's more appropriate to compare it to the temperature of the human body than to the normal fluctuations we experience in weather. A 2-degree temperature rise in a human being is a fever. A rise of 5 or 6 degrees centigrade—the increase we can expect if greenhouse gas emissions go unabated—is fatal.

To keep atmospheric temperature rise below 2 degrees centigrade, the Intergovernmental Panel on Climate Change (IPCC), a collection of the world's top scientists, says that global carbon dioxide emissions must peak within the next few years and begin to decline. Most experts accept that industrial nations must take most of the responsibility for reducing greenhouse gas emissions, at least over the next few decades. After all, the industrialized nations account for most of the man-made greenhouse gases in the atmosphere today, and have greater resources to address the challenges they've produced. In August 2007, a group of 158 nations meeting on the climate problem urged industrialized economies to reduce their emissions as much as 40 percent by 2020, compared to 1990 levels.

But the trend is moving rapidly in the opposite direction. Here in the United States, the nation most responsible for the current atmospheric concentrations of greenhouse gases, the Energy Information Administration predicts that if we continue business as usual, our emissions will not stabilize and decline; they'll grow 35 percent by 2030. If global emissions continue unabated, carbon dioxide concentrations in the atmosphere will be double preindustrial levels by midcentury.

Today, signs of climate change are appearing much more quickly than predicted and they are not restricted to the Arctic and Antarctic. Troubling patterns are emerging in the United States.* For example:

- In the far west, wildfires are regularly setting new records for their size and intensity. The National Oceanic and Atmospheric Administration reported in 2007 that the 2006 wildfire season in the United States set an all-time record with more than 9.8 million acres burned in more than 96,000 wildfires. The National Interagency Fire Center reports that nearly 14,000 square miles burned in 2007, costing the federal government more than $1.8 billion and making the year the second-costliest fire season on record.

---

* To see how climate change is already manifesting in the United States and around the world, see this great animation at Google Earth.

- During 2008, nuclear power plants in the southeastern United States faced the prospect of curtailing generation because a prolonged drought in that region left them with insufficient water to cool their reactors. Drought is becoming a factor in the power choices of other regions, too.

- On September 1, 2008, New Orleans was evacuated as Hurricane Gustav threatened it and other areas of the Gulf Coast. Gustav appeared almost exactly on the third anniversary of the city's devastation from Hurricane Katrina. It was followed quickly by Hurricane Ike, which caused billions of dollars' worth of damage when it hit the Texas coast and traveled deep into the U.S. mainland. Seven of the ten most expensive hurricanes on record have occurred since 2004.

- The nation's flood season started unusually early in 2008. Flooding in March killed at least sixteen people in Missouri, Arkansas, Tennessee, and Oklahoma. In the Midwest, severe flooding started even before winter was over as heavy snow alternated with warm weather. The Mississippi River was so swollen from March floods that officials talked about diverting water from the river into Lake Pontchartrain—the lake that flooded New Orleans after Hurricane Katrina.

Climate scientists are reluctant to attribute single weather events, or even short-term weather patterns, to global climate change. But a growing number of experts are acknowledging that these extreme events may be the early signs of impacts that will grow much, much worse.

In other words, we can't leave global warming to be solved by future generations. The problem is here and now. Solving it will require nothing less than a transformation in how we and the world's other people fuel our prosperity—a change in which we finally make economic development compatible with environmental protection and restoration.

2.

Great Challenges, Great Opportunities

If global climate change is the greatest challenge of our era, it also is the greatest opportunity. As former President Bill Clinton puts it, "Creating the low-carbon economy will lead to the greatest economic boom in the United States since we mobilized for World War II." And that might be understating the potential of this moment.

Global warming is a signal that our old economy no longer works. It's not the only sign of malfunction. As I write this, the Department of Labor reports that 9.4 million Americans are unemployed and 84,000 jobs disappeared in just one month. The Economic Policy Institute (EPI) reports that "working families are seeing extraordinary economic challenges." In its 2008/2009 State of Working America analysis, EPI writes:

> When it comes to efficient, profitable production, the men
> and women of the American workforce have a lot to be proud
> of. But when it comes to being rewarded for the work they do,
> the skills they have sharpened, and the contributions they
> make . . . well, that's a different story. Their paychecks have
> been frozen, their health coverage is being cut back, their jobs
> are at risk of being shipped overseas, and their pensions are

more precarious than ever. For the first time since the Census Bureau began tracking such data back in the mid-1940s, the real incomes of middle-class families are lower at the end of this business cycle than they were when it started. This fact stands as the single most compelling piece of evidence that prosperity is eluding working families.

The overriding responsibility facing the next President is to lead the United States, and to assist the rest of the world, in creating a new economy that delivers prosperity in the new realities of the twenty-first century. What are those realities?

First, more nations, including the world's largest, are committed to intense economic development to lift their people out of poverty. That means more cars, more buildings, more appliances, more energy consumption, more pollution, and more climate change, if the emerging economies follow the same path the industrialized world followed, including conspicuous consumption, careless waste of resources, environmental degradation, and intensive use of fossil energy. Left unaddressed, the negative impacts of global climate change will increasingly tax prosperity.

Second, the growing economies and the growing world population—scheduled to increase from 6.5 billion to 9 billion by midcentury—are creating competition for oil and natural gas at the same time global supplies of those finite fuels are peaking or in decline. There are two results: oil and gas prices are rising as demand exceeds supplies, and competition for the fuels is adding to international tensions. In the old international order, when nations demanded more petroleum, the world responded by producing it. Today, the global oil market has become a zero-sum game. When one nation obtains more oil, other nations obtain less, and U.S. intelligence experts predict more conflicts ahead.

Third, we have reached the limits of the environment's ability to absorb the impact of carbon economies. In the old days, environmental problems seemed local—a burning river, a degraded forest, a polluted waterway, a regional threat to air quality. Today, we know we are threatening the quality of the earth's life-support systems—the atmosphere, forests, and oceans. The carbon emissions from each household, factory, automobile, and city affect all people everywhere. Spaceship Earth is becoming Greenhouse Earth and global warming has become perverse evidence that we are all, indeed, interconnected.

Fourth, as Vietnam showed us a generation ago and as the war in Iraq has demonstrated today, the nature of warfare has changed. Fielding the biggest armies with the most modern weapons can no longer guarantee access to natural resources. As one observer has put it, when you've used up all your capital you can do one of two things: declare bankruptcy or pick up your gun and rob a bank. The United States has used up all of its easy carbon capital. Oil and gas production peaked here in the early 1970s. But the modern reality of asymmetric warfare, where an inferior but determined enemy can cause such high losses of life and treasure that a militarily superior nation loses the will to fight, has made "robbing the bank" not only morally wrong, but also too costly and too uncertain. And where the "bank" is located in sensitive places such as Islamic holy lands, staking it out fuels terrorism.

The United States and other industrialized nations must decarbonize their economies and do so quickly, in the process demonstrating a new path to prosperity for developing countries. At the core of the transformation will be the switch from finite, carbon-intensive fuels to resource-efficient economies powered by renewable low- and no-carbon fuels. We have all the technologies and knowledge we need. We know, for example, how to produce energy from sunlight, wind, geothermal resources, and biomass materials. The technology exists for much more efficient vehicles, buildings, and power production. We don't lack technology; we have lacked the political will to use it.

But that is changing. The promising early evidence of the post-carbon economy already is appearing. Since 1974, the world's sixth largest economy—the state of California—has held its population's energy consumption to zero growth while energy consumption in the rest of the United States grew 50 percent. The state's per capita greenhouse gas emissions have fallen 30 percent since 1975. By one estimate, the average family in California has been paying eight hundred dollars less for energy each year than it would have without the state's energy efficiency efforts—and that was before the recent surge in oil prices.

In Texas, legislators implemented a requirement in 1999 that part of the state's electricity must come from renewable resources—a mandate known as a renewable energy portfolio standard, or RPS. The state met its ten-year goal in only six years. Today, Texas is the nation's largest producer of wind power and it recently approved the nation's largest investment in renewable energy to date—$4.9 billion to extend the electric grid to new wind resources.

In Colorado, proposals for an RPS failed year after year in the state legislature because of opposition from utilities, including the state's largest, Xcel Energy. In 2004, voters took matters into their own hands and passed the nation's first ballot initiative establishing an RPS. It required utilities to obtain 10 percent of their electricity from renewable resources in ten years. But wind and solar power grew so fast that the legislature doubled the standard three years later, requiring the state's large utilities to obtain 20 percent of their electricity from renewables by 2020. An economic analysis predicted the state's gross domestic product would increase by

$1.9 billion under the new requirement, and this time it passed in the legislature with Xcel Energy's support. Today, renewable energy portfolio requirements have been established in thirty-two states and the District of Columbia.

In 2006, Colorado Governor Bill Ritter won the election by promising to lead the state to a "new energy economy." Attracted by that plan and by the state's renewable energy mandate, the Danish wind company Vestas is building four manufacturing plants in Colorado to produce wind turbine blades and towers. The plants will create 2,450 green jobs. More and more blueprints are emerging for how the rest of America can create a new energy economy. The Apollo Alliance, a coalition of business, labor, environmental, and community leaders, has developed a plan to create 5 million high-quality "green-collar" jobs with an investment of $500 billion over ten years; the Center for American Progress has developed a road map to the new economy and an analysis that shows, state by state, how an investment of $100 billion over two years would create 2 million good jobs.

Amid all the bad news in the economy as the 2008 presidential election approaches, it is easy to miss the other good news that a sustainable economy is emerging. For example:

- The U.S. Department of Energy (DOE) reports that renewable energy technologies are booming worldwide. The number of renewable energy installations in the world and the United States doubled between 2000 and 2007. During the same period, worldwide wind energy generation quadrupled and installed wind capacity in the United States increased six and a half times.

- DOE says that U.S. investments in renewable energy projects grew dramatically over the past decade, reaching more than

$13 billion in 2007. Investments in wind energy projects grew from $250 million in 2001 to more than $8 billion in 2007. During the same period, venture capital investments in solar technology increased from $5 million to more than $1 billion.

- The United Nations reports that the global market for environmental products and services is projected to double from $1.37 trillion per year at present to $2.74 trillion by 2020.

- An estimated 2.3 million people worldwide have found new jobs in the renewable energy sector, the UN says. It estimates that the number of jobs in wind power will rise to 2.1 million and jobs in solar energy will grow to 6.3 million by 2030.

- Improving the energy efficiency of buildings could generate as many as 3.5 million green jobs in Europe and the United States, with much higher potential in developing countries.

- The world economy is beginning to produce "solar billionaires." There are at least three today: Shi Zhengrong of China, founder of Suntech Power Holdings Company; Frank Asbeck, founder of Germany's SolarWorld; and Xiaofeng Peng, head of LDK Solar in China.

- The demand for hybrid and fuel-efficient cars has increased so rapidly that General Motors is in a race with Toyota to produce market-ready next-generation electric vehicles by the end of this decade. Ford has announced it's converting two of its manufacturing plants from trucks—previously its bestseller—to the production of more fuel-efficient cars.

- Two of America's most successful oil tycoons now are betting on renewable energy. T. Boone Pickens is building the world's largest wind farm in Texas and is buying $58 million in TV time to tell America that we can't "drill our way out" of the energy crisis. Denver billionaire Philip Anschutz is developing a two-thousand-megawatt wind project in Wyoming and has acquired rights to build a $3 billion, nine-hundred-mile transmission project that will move wind-generated power to Southern California, Las Vegas, and Phoenix.

- Shareholders in America's big oil companies—for example, members of the Rockefeller family whose forebears founded what is now Exxon Mobil—are pressuring CEOs to invest more in the renewable energy resources of tomorrow. (While a few oil companies such as British Petroleum are investing in renewables today, those investments reportedly amount to less than 1 percent of their capital spending.)

- Wind is making money for lesser tycoons, too. Farmers, ranchers, and communities in rural America are discovering that the wind is a lucrative cash crop. Farmers are leasing sites for wind turbines at thousands of dollars per turbine per year. Wind power is generating new income for states and localities, too. GE Energy Financial Services estimates that wind projects capable of generating five thousand megawatts of electricity went on line in the United States last year. The plants are providing $6 million annually in local property taxes, $15 million annually in state income taxes, 17,000 construction-related jobs, and 1,600 long-term jobs. Although wind power provides only about 1 percent of America's electricity today, the U.S. Department of Energy says it can provide 20 percent of our power in the years ahead.

- The future is just as bright for solar power. McKinsey & Company, the respected global consulting firm, predicts that over the next three to seven years, the unsubsidized cost of solar energy will compete with conventional electricity in California and the southwestern United States. The company projects that solar electricity will cost as little as ten cents a kilowatt-hour by 2020, down from thirty-six cents today.

Investing in the Future

The transition to the twenty-first century economy won't be cheap. It will require massive public and private investments. For example, DOE figures it would cost at least $43 billion to obtain 20 percent of the nation's projected electric demand from wind power by 2030.

Billions of dollars in public and private investment will be needed to upgrade the nation's aging electric infrastructure so that it is more reliable and efficient and able to more effectively move solar and wind energy around the country.

Other types of infrastructure also need upgrading. Today, America is investing only 2.4 percent of its gross domestic product in infrastructure—half of Europe's investment rate, and only a third of China's. The American Society of Civil Engineers has estimated that $1.6 trillion is required nationwide for infrastructure repairs. A national commission estimates that the U.S. government should invest at least $225 billion each year for the next fifty years to modernize our transportation systems. The U.S. Environmental Protection Agency estimates that the nation needs to spend $11 billion more each year over the next twenty years to fix our water systems.

But these are investments America cannot afford to avoid. Our national objective should be to channel public and private capital to the technologies that will unleash the new economy. Without forward-looking investment, the United States will have runaway carbon emissions and the infrastructure of a third-world country, threatening public safety and stunting our economic growth. For example, flight delays are costing at least $15 billion each year; traffic congestion costs $78 billion annually. Inefficient buildings are causing an estimated $58 billion annually in worker sick time. Extreme weather events caused losses of about $50 billion world-wide in the first half of 2008, and that trend is expected to become the new norm as a result of climate change.

On the other hand, a campaign to rebuild America's infrastructure would create 47,500 jobs for every $1 billion invested while providing the opportunity to make our roads, bridges, electric grid, and waterworks more resilient against the predicted impacts of climate change. These are jobs that can't be exported overseas.

The best-available green building technologies could increase labor productivity by $200 billion each year. If Pickens is correct, clean, domestic energy technologies will help prevent the transfer of $10 trillion out of the U.S. economy over the next decade—the hemorrhage he estimates we'll experience if we continue import-ing oil at current levels and prices. And by emphasizing the use of low-carbon and environmentally friendly materials, an effort to rebuild America would create new green jobs and new markets for the green products that will support the twenty-first century economy.

The Time Is Now

The new President must make economic transformation an urgent national mission and must rally Congress, business, private in-vestors, and state and local government officials to join the cam-paign. There is no more time to lose. Each year we postpone the transition, the window of opportunity closes farther as American competitiveness declines, the costs of climate change and fossil energy dependence grow, and other nations capture the huge global market for clean technologies. The President should:

- Use state-of-the-art communications technology to engage the nation in a conversation about the future. New technologies are available to hold National Town Meetings that help citizens envision what a postcarbon America would be like—homes, workplaces, vehicles, communities. Millions of Americans can engage in real-time voting on their preferences, using available computer equipment. To win broad support for economic transformation, the administration can help the American people own the vision of that positive new society, and to own it they must help create it.

- Establish an Energy Security and Climate Stabilization Board consisting of America's top academic, financial, corporate, nonprofit, and government leaders, and charge the board with framing a road map to the new economy. The board would be a cross between President Roosevelt's War Production Board created in 1942 "for the purpose of assuring the most effective prosecution of war procurement and production," and President Clinton's President's Council on Sustainable Development. The board should recommend the market mechanisms, regulatory reforms, trade policies, and barrier-busting initiatives that will unleash economic transformation.

- Direct that where they have the legal authority to do so, agencies should retarget their grant, loan, and loan guarantee programs to capitalize low-carbon buildings, vehicles, communities, and energy systems. The loan guarantee programs administered by the Department of Energy and the Department of Agriculture's Rural Utility Service, for example, should give highest, and perhaps exclusive, priority to renewable energy projects. Where legal authority for retargeting does not now exist, the administration should work closely with Congress to ensure that taxpayer investments in infrastructure serve the new economy, not the old one.

- Champion innovation and small business development. The President should propose that $1 billion be allocated over five years to provide "platinum carrot" awards for breakthroughs in transformative technologies such as better batteries, plug-in hybrid vehicles, and ethanol made from nonfood crops. Because small businesses are America's principal source of new jobs and patents, the President should direct the U.S. Small Business Administration to beef up its programs to help veterans, women, and minorities start green enterprises.

- Direct agencies to use their power as consumers to open new markets for green products, from paper and paper clips to trucks and tanks. With more than 500,000 buildings, 600,000 vehicles, and $18 billion in energy expenditures each year, the federal government can become a huge, sustained customer for green energy and products, spurring industries to invest in new plants and equipment. The government can require that its supply chains comply with standards to reduce their carbon footprints; it can require that state and local agencies do the same when they receive federal funding.

In a recent report, the McKinsey Global Institute concluded that to achieve necessary reductions in carbon emissions while maintaining economic growth, the world needs a "carbon revolution" comparable to the Industrial Revolution—but in one-third the time. The costs are manageable and we have the technologies we need, the institute said.

We also have the talent. The Brookings Institution confirms that although America's global leadership in innovation is slipping, we are still the world's innovation leader, producing far more patents, employing more Nobel Laureates, and boasting more top universities than any other nation. A growing number of U.S. businesses, including some of the nation's largest corporations, are moving ahead with climate action.

This is a time that merits superlatives. It is a moment of extraordinary opportunity, arguably the greatest challenge yet for America's genius and entrepreneurial spirit. It tests our character and our commitment to the nation's future.

To pass the test and capture the opportunity, we must meet the job of economic transformation head-on. We need new policies and institutions, smart investments, and a national commitment for change. And we need elected leaders who are willing to help the nation step boldly into this new century.

3.

The Great Trap: Carbon Lock-In

A critical step in reversing global climate change is to prevent "carbon lock-in," the construction of coal-fired power plants, inefficient buildings, and gas-guzzling vehicles that commit the nation to decades of more greenhouse gas emissions. The typical power plant remains in service for forty to sixty years; the typical building for about forty years; the average vehicle thirteen to fifteen years and 145,000 miles.

If we continue building as we have done in the past, the best we can hope for is an Alice in Wonderland world where "it takes all the running you can do, to keep in the same place." Architect Ed Mazria, who is rallying America's building industry around the goal of zero-carbon buildings, points out that if every household in the United States joined the climate-action effort by changing one sixty-watt incandescent lightbulb to a compact fluorescent, two new coal plants would completely negate the effort.

More likely, carbon lock-in would push us backward to an atmospheric carbon debt we will never be able to repay. "Carbon dioxide (CO_2) and other heat-trapping gases persist in the atmosphere for centuries, so decisions made in the next five to ten years will alter the Earth's climate for generations to come. Our best hope for staying in the game is to limit new sources of greenhouse gases so that technological breakthroughs can save us down the line," according to "Design to Win: Philanthropy's Role in the Fight Against Global Warming," a 2007 report written by California Environmental Associates. "New factories, offices, stores, and homes threaten to lock-in still more carbon emissions if they're not designed correctly. In some cases, retrofits and updates can ameliorate the impact—but at a steep price. . . . Each year the status quo persists, the task gets tougher: the amount of emissions reduction needed will rise; at the same time, the share of mitigation we can identify will fall. If we don't immediately confront lock-in, even a dramatic scale-up of emissions-free technologies, such as wind and solar, won't allow us to catch a train that's leaving the station—and picking up steam."

The following are five steps that must be taken to reduce lock-in.

Ban Construction of New Coal-Fired Power Plants Not Able to Capture and Store Greenhouse Gas Emissions

The generation of electric power accounts for nearly 40 percent of America's greenhouse gas emissions today, mostly from coal, the dirtiest of the fossil fuels. A moratorium on conventional coal power plants is the single most important action necessary to prevent more carbon debt. In May 2007, the U.S. Department of Energy reported that 151 new coal-fired power plants were proposed or in various stages of construction in the United States. Each would be a significant setback to our efforts to fight climate change.

Consumers, states, and investors are taking action. By the fall of 2008, more than eighty of the new plants reportedly had been stopped by legal action, by the difficulty of finding capital because investors are worried about the future economics of coal, or by state officials wanting to limit greenhouse gas emissions and other pollutants. But without a nationwide ban, some new conventional coal plants will be built, each representing a case of carbon lock-in. A federal ban would eliminate uncertainty in the power market, and encourage utilities and investors to move more rapidly to cleaner forms of electricity.

How will we be able to produce the electric power we need? The simple answer is that it doesn't need to come from coal. The American Solar Energy Society, the Nuclear Policy Institute, and the Institute for Energy and Environmental Research have all concluded that U.S. electric demand in the decades ahead can be met with a combination of energy efficiency and renewable energy technologies, and without new nuclear or coal power plants.

A reminder: The United States can't conquer power plant lock-in alone. Coal supplies are cheap and abundant around the world and many nations are planning to use them. Thirty-seven nations reportedly are planning new coal power plants over the next five years. China is building the equivalent of one to two five-hundred-megawatt coal plants every *week*. Coal is one of the reasons that international collaboration will be vital in the fight against global warming.

Increase the CAFE (Corporate Average Fuel Efficiency) Standard

The transportation sector—planes, trains, and motor vehicles—is responsible for most of the oil we import and consume in the United States. The sector is also responsible for 34 percent of U.S. greenhouse gas emissions. In 1984, after the Arab oil embargoes of the 1970s, Congress created the CAFE standard, requiring that automakers produce vehicles that achieve a fleet-wide average of at least 27.5 miles per gallon. That standard remained unchanged for twenty-four years; it finally was increased by Congress in

December 2007. Now, automakers must achieve a fleet-wide average of thirty-five miles per gallon by 2020.

That's not nearly enough. Japan's standard is already forty-seven miles per gallon; Europe's is being raised to forty-nine miles per gallon. Vehicles on U.S. highways today are able to exceed fifty miles per gallon. Because reducing oil consumption is a national security imperative as well as necessary for climate stabilization, the President should propose that the CAFE standard be increased to at least fifty miles per gallon by 2020 and to two hundred miles per gallon by 2050. How can we talk about *two hundred miles per gallon* when U.S. auto manufacturers say it will be difficult to meet the current standard? Older Americans will remember how, under FDR's leadership, U.S. automakers quickly retooled their manufacturing plants to make tanks and aircraft during World War II. Climate change requires just such an effort. Besides, advancements in nonpetroleum vehicles by 2050 will make the two-hundred-mile-per-gallon goal much easier to achieve.

At the same time, the President and Congress should provide sufficient research funds to speed the development of low-carbon, nonpetroleum fuels such as ethanol made from nonfood crops and urban wastes.

Increase Transportation Efficiency in Urban Areas

We must begin to provide people with more options to their single-occupancy cars and SUVs. Reducing "vehicle miles traveled" is as important as new vehicle and fuel technologies to reducing carbon emissions and ending oil imports. One opportunity will be the reauthorization of the federal transportation bill, which comes before Congress in 2009. The President can do the following:

- Encourage Congress to reform transportation funding for states and localities. PCAP has produced a long list of detailed recommendations on how to shift priorities from highway construction to mass transit, incentives for ride-sharing, safe accommodations for pedestrians and bicyclists, and the development of high-speed rail for intercity travel.

- Direct the Environmental Protection Agency to intensify its financial and technical programs to help communities engage in "smart growth"—denser, mixed-use, and transit-oriented development.

Develop and Create Incentives for States to Adopt Aggressive New Codes for Residential and Commercial Buildings

The nation's 116 million homes and approximately 5 million commercial buildings use nearly 40 percent of our energy and emit 38.5 percent of our greenhouse gas emissions. We need aggressive new building codes to ensure that every new commercial and residential building in the United States is carbon-neutral by 2030.

It is already possible to build homes and commercial buildings that produce no net greenhouse gas emissions. The key is high levels of efficiency in the building and its equipment, combined with solar panels and other on-site energy systems that produce as much or more energy than the building consumes each year. The American Solar Energy Society predicts that these zero-energy buildings will be cost-competitive alternatives in the marketplace by 2020. Many of them will be *selling* power to electric utilities rather than buying it.

To achieve this goal, the President should:

- Urge Congress to extend energy-efficiency and renewable energy tax incentives to 2020.

- Create new model national building codes for zero-carbon residential and commercial buildings, and provide incentives for states to adopt the codes as soon as possible. DOE works with the building industry to create and periodically update model building codes. It is up to states and localities to adopt and enforce the codes. DOE should develop advanced model codes for carbon-neutral buildings and use the State Energy Program, which provides energy grants to states, to reward early adopters.

Regulate Greenhouse Gases Under the Clean Air Act

Whatever the prospects for a carbon-pricing bill from Congress, the President should urge the administrator of the U.S. Environmental Protection Agency to immediately begin regulating greenhouse gas emissions under the Clean Air Act—something the U.S. Supreme Court has ruled EPA can do.

In the Bush administration, the EPA administrator stalled on regulation. The new President can only encourage fast action, because Congress has delegated the regulatory authority to EPA. But the President can make the new administrator's commitment to regulation part of the job interview.

Using the Clean Air Act is important for several reasons. First, we don't know if or when Congress will pass a cap-and-trade system (see Chapter 4) that the administration can then implement. Congressional passage remains uncertain and the rulemaking process used by agencies can take many months. It may take additional time to find the right carbon cap and price.

Second, some experts believe the United States should not approve or implement a cap-and-trade regime until it's clear what the international scheme will be for reducing global emissions. Nations will gather in Copenhagen in December 2009 to discuss an agreement to succeed the Kyoto Protocol and it's difficult to predict how long it will be before such an agreement is in place. It would be impolitic, some observers feel, for the United States to show up with its own scheme, particularly if it may not be compatible with international efforts.

While these developments are sorted out, the United States must begin making progress on curbing carbon emissions. Clean Air Act regulation can accomplish that. If and when carbon pricing is in place and functioning well, any duplicative portions of the regulatory regime will become moot.

Besides, when it comes to an issue as important as global warming, some duplication of government effort is not necessarily a sin.

4.

Mobilizing the Marketplace

Whatever their philosophy of government, most leaders now agree that we must mobilize the American marketplace to help deal with climate change. Today, the touted "magic of the marketplace" doesn't exist in regard to greenhouse gas emissions. Indeed, British economist Sir Nicholas Stern, former chief economist for the World Bank, calls global climate change "a result of the greatest market failure the world has seen."

The reason is simple: When we buy a gallon of gasoline or pay for a kilowatt-hour of electricity, the price does not reflect the true cost of those products. It does not count, for example, the damage done by the carbon dioxide the gasoline emits when we burn it, or the CO_2 produced by the coal-fired power plant that provides our electricity.

To correct this problem, national policy makers are considering at least two approaches. The first, said to be favored by most economists, is to add a carbon tax to gasoline, electricity, and other products responsible for carbon emissions. The second approach, favored by most politicians because they fear a voter backlash against any new tax, is known as "cap and trade." In this approach, the federal government would establish a cap on national greenhouse gas emissions. Then, it would auction pollution permits, or allowances, to big carbon emitters. Those whose emissions are below their allowances could sell their unused portion to those whose emissions are too high.

Let's say, for example, that Congress has decided there should only be one thousand pennies circulating in the national economy. In order to have pennies, you must buy an allowance from the government. You purchase an allowance for ten pennies. If you actually have only five pennies, you can sell the allowance for your other five to someone else who has more pennies than his allowance. In other words, he could have fifteen pennies so long as he purchased the right to five extra, and you would earn money by selling your allowance to him. Meanwhile, the number of pennies in circulation remains the same.

If this sounds complicated, it is. But the expected result is twofold. First, the system would establish a firm limit on the nation's carbon emissions—a limit that would decrease every year. Second, cap-and-trade would produce significant revenues for the government to invest in clean technologies, in helping people cope with climate change, or in other objectives. Estimates are that those revenues could be $100 billion to $200 billion the first year and would grow each year the system is in place.

For U.S. consumers, the result would be higher prices for carbon-intensive fuels and products. Electricity would cost more if it's generated from coal. Gasoline would cost more, too. When that happens, the marketplace will send more accurate signals about the full costs of carbon-based fuels and products, encouraging consumers to conserve, to become more efficient, or to buy fuels and products that emit fewer greenhouse gases. Eventually, solar and wind power and low-carbon biofuels will be cheaper than conventional carbon-based energy. In the meantime, consumers can take aggressive energy efficiency measures to help them cope with higher fossil fuel costs.

The first bill to create a cap-and-trade system was introduced in 2003 by Senators John McCain and Joe Lieberman. Many other bills have followed, including several that would lead to even greater cuts in emissions, but Congress has yet to even vote on the idea. No matter the mechanism Congress ultimately chooses, putting a price on carbon is an essential step to mobilizing the marketplace for reducing greenhouse gases.

However, this first step won't be fully effective without a second step that may be even more difficult for Congress: ending public subsidies that promote greenhouse gas emissions, including tens of billions of dollars that go each year to the coal, oil, and natural gas industries.

These actions require legislation in Congress, but the President can use his veto power and his influence to help shape the outcome. The following are some examples of what can be done.

Trading Upstream

There are several important questions involved in designing an effective cap-and-trade system. Should the federal government give some of the allowances away, or should 100 percent of them be auctioned? Should there be a so-called safety valve that limits how high carbon prices will go? To whom should the allowances be sold?

To understand this last issue, think of the nation's conventional energy supply as a stream. At the top of the stream are the companies that bring fossil fuels into the economy by mining coal, drilling for oil and natural gas, or importing fossil fuels from other nations. Midway down the stream are the entities that emit carbon by burning these fuels—power plants and large industries, for example. Downstream are individual consumers, such as home and car owners.

Most bills in Congress would sell emission allowances midstream, to utilities and industries. But Yale economist Dr. Robert Repetto, commissioned by PCAP to study these questions, argues that allowances should be sold upstream to those who produce fossil fuels. The architecture of cap-and-trade is important, Repetto says, because if Congress gets it wrong, the costs will be enormous. "Over a decade, the excess cost of an inferior policy choice could be $1.75 trillion or more, given the annual growth in the economy," he concludes. "This would be enough to resolve the social security shortfall, fund expanded health care coverage, eliminate the budget deficit, or fulfill many other worthy public goals."

Repetto's upstream approach would be far simpler and cheaper to administer. It would involve emission allowances to only about two thousand entities, rather than the tens of thousands of power plants and industries at midstream. Because it would be so much simpler, the upstream approach would be more transparent and more difficult to cheat.

Critics of Repetto's approach argue that cap-and-trade will be more successful if power plants and industries are allowed to buy and sell pollution allowances. The potential for profit will make them more aggressive at saving energy and backing new technologies, this argument goes. Midstream backers also argue that because there are more utilities and industries than there are energy companies, a midstream system would have more supporters in Congress.

However, the upstream approach has another important advantage: It would lead to emission reductions across the entire economy. When coal, oil, and gas producers purchase emission permits, they will add those costs to the price of their fuels. The effect of carbon pricing would trickle down to every place that oil, coal, and gas are consumed, covering even hard-to-reach sectors such as transportation and agriculture.

Whatever system of carbon pricing Congress chooses, however, the President should insist that it meet a number of criteria to earn his signature. It should:

- Cover all six greenhouse gases.
- Produce emission reductions of at least 80 percent below 1990 levels by 2050, and at least 30 percent by 2020.
- Sell 100 percent of the emission allowances, and not give any away.
- Be transparent, simple, and relatively inexpensive to administer.
- Cover the entire economy.
- Be flexible, with some mechanism to regularly review performance and adjust carbon caps without requiring further Congressional action.
- Be compatible with whatever international carbon control mechanism the international community develops to succeed the Kyoto Protocol.
- Measure carbon reductions in absolute tons rather than in carbon intensity (emissions per dollar of gross domestic product). Absolute reductions are required to bring climate change under control.
- Reward early adopters.
- Distribute revenues in three ways: Some should be returned to every American in the form of tax reductions or dividends, underscoring the principle that the atmosphere belongs to us all and we all benefit from its protection. Some should be used to create long-term energy savings for all consumers through greater energy efficiency and the development of low-carbon energy technologies. A third portion should be used to help consumers, companies, and communities least able to cope with the adverse impacts of climate change or climate policy.

As I have said, the transition to a postcarbon economy will require major investments, including many identified in the Presidential Climate Action Plan. But the President, Congress, and taxpayers should not regard revenues from carbon pricing as the only source of public money for the transition to a low-carbon economy. That leads to the issue of subsidies.

Stop Subsidizing Carbon

In ways that are both obvious and subtle, we are paying one another to change the climate. The President should lead an effort to "decarbonize" the public subsidy system at all levels—local, state, national, and international.

The first step, mentioned earlier, is to end federal subsidies for oil, natural gas, and coal. They are mature, well-established, and well-financed industries that, national subsidy expert Doug Koplow estimates, receive about $50 billion annually in public largesse. Public subsidies in the form of tax breaks, low royalty and lease payments for production on public lands, and research dollars, for example, are classic corporate welfare. If taxpayers are to subsidize energy, it should be those emerging industries we need to reduce carbon emissions, including young renewable energy and energy efficiency technologies under development or struggling to survive the "valley of death"—the gap between the laboratory and the marketplace.

Another important reason to end fossil fuel subsidies is that they work against the objective of carbon pricing. It makes no sense to correct market signals with a carbon tax or with cap-and-trade, while continuing to distort market signals with subsidies.

The President should encourage states and localities to follow the federal example. Koplow estimates that combined federal, state, and local subsidies for fossil energy could be in the range of hundreds of billions of dollars each year—an enormous resource that could and should be redirected to the energy technologies we need for a twenty-first century economy.

Next, the President should lead an effort to reform other federal subsidies that encourage global warming. Koplow points out that there has never been an inventory of federal carbon subsidies, including tax provisions, research grants, loans, loan guarantees, and direct expenditures. The President should direct the Office of Management and Budget to conduct such an inventory and publish it on the Internet.

When that's been done, the President should appoint a Presidential Commission on Carbon Subsidy Reform to recommend which of the subsidies can be terminated without undermining national security or economic stability. Subsidy reform will be highly controversial. For example, the home mortgage interest deduction encourages the construction of larger homes—one of the factors the U.S. Energy Information Administration says is driving up energy use and greenhouse gas emissions. In the 110th Congress, Representative John Dingell proposed that this tax benefit be reduced for homes of 3,000 square feet and larger, and eliminated entirely for homes of more than 4,200 square feet. Big homes would continue to qualify for the deduction if they met high standards for energy efficiency. Homebuilders, the mortgage industry, and McMansion owners undoubtedly would fight hard to keep their subsidy.

The commission could handle the controversy by recommending an all-or-nothing package of subsidy reforms, in the same way that past commissions have recommended military base closings. Congress would vote the entire package up or down, rather than picking winners and losers. The purpose of the exercise would not be to stroll into the pasture and start indiscriminately shooting sacred cows. The purpose would be to cull the herd of those that are significant barriers to the goal of mitigating climate change.

Finally, the President should charge the commission with proposing reforms in how and why subsidies are granted in the future. For example, taxpayer support should be given only to those resources, technologies, or activities that have positive benefits for the economy, environment, energy security, and climate stabilization. Those benefits should be measured over the life cycles of subsidized resources and should count full costs. For example, an ethanol plant might deserve public subsidy; an ethanol plant that obtains its process heat from coal would not. Subsidy levels for a given technology should decline over time to encourage early progress. At the same time, subsidies should last long enough to create a stable environment for private investment. (In the past, Congress has created boom-bust cycles in the solar and wind industries by forcing tax credits to be reauthorized every two years, creating uncertainty for investors.)

For too long and in too many cases, public subsidies have been driven by powerful lobbies rather than by good public policy. If we really want the marketplace to be our ally in stabilizing the climate, energy prices, and national security, then we should create good market signals and eliminate the perverse ones.

5.

Restore the Integrity of Climate Science

We need the best possible science and technology to conquer the complex problem of climate change. We must continuously improve our understanding of the earth's environment and its life-support systems, and we must strive for new technologies that reduce civilization's carbon footprint. Few institutions in the world are better equipped to help than the U.S. government.

Some 100,000 scientists and engineers are employed by the federal government, working in agencies and in seven hundred research institutions.* Thirteen federal agencies participate in the federal Climate Change Science Program (CCSP). Its mission is to better understand the causes and effects of global warming and to provide that critical information to decision-makers in the United States and around the world.

---

* Government research facilities include nine world-class national laboratories: Argonne National Laboratory, Argonne, IL; Brookhaven National Laboratory, Upton, NY; Idaho National Laboratory, Idaho Falls, ID; Lawrence Berkeley National Laboratory, Berkeley, CA; Lawrence Livermore National Laboratory, Livermore, CA; Los Alamos National Laboratory, Los Alamos, NM; Oak Ridge National Laboratory, Oak Ridge, TN; Pacific Northwest National Laboratory, Richland, WA; Sandia National Laboratories, Albuquerque, NM.

How important is the government's research? "Federal climate science research is at the forefront of assessing fundamental causes of global warming and the future dangers it could pose to our nation and the world," according to the Union of Concerned Scientists. "Such research is of tremendous value to many Americans planning for these risks, including coastal communities designing infrastructure for protecting against storm surges; civil authorities planning for heat waves; power companies preparing for higher peak energy demands; forest managers planning wildfire management programs; ski resort owners investing in snow-making equipment; and policy makers evaluating energy legislation."

During the past eight years, however, the Bush administration has systematically undermined the strength and integrity of federal climate science. The administration filled key positions with lobbyists from the fossil energy industries; authorized them to edit and censor scientific reports; shifted money from earth sciences to the President's Mission to Mars program; failed to meet congressional deadlines for scientific reports; and even deleted the phrase "understand and protect the home planet" from the mission statement of the National Aeronautic and Space Administration (NASA).

In one case, an oil industry lobbyist hired by the White House was caught changing the key conclusions of scientific reports on climate change. He resigned and went back to the oil industry. In another case, the White House refused to open an e-mail from the U.S. Environmental Protection Agency to avoid its conclusions. "The President simply didn't want to know information that ran contrary to his intention to serve the fossil energy industries," one prominent scientist told us. Interference also has been reported in science related to endangered species and to identifying cancer-causing pollutants.*

The Congressional Research Service (CRS) reports that since 2005, funding for climate change research and analysis at NASA has declined. The National Center for Atmospheric Research—one of the U.S. institutions that participated in the IPCC's Nobel Prize–winning studies—announced in August 2008 that budget cuts had forced it to shut down a program designed to help poor countries anticipate and survive droughts, floods, and other severe impacts of climate change. The program was terminated just two months after the National Intelligence Council issued an assessment that climate change is a serious threat to U.S. national security, in part because of the disruptions it will cause in those same impoverished and volatile regions.

Today, 70 percent of American adults believe the United States is no longer a world leader in scientific achievement and the integrity of federal science is in question. As a scientist at NASA has put it: "Politicizing and degrading the integrity for which we are internationally known and respected is a disservice to our country and a danger to the world. If we can't be trusted to give insights on global change and funded to do so, who in the world will do it."

The next President must reestablish the credibility, reputation, and resources of federal science programs, most urgently those that help us understand and find solutions to climate change. The following are some examples of what this will include.

---

* For more detail on problems with and solutions for federal science, see "After Bush, Restoring Science to Environmental Policy," Chris Mooney. Also see "Atmosphere of Pressure: Political Interference in Federal Climate Science," Union of Concerned Scientists and the Government Accountability Project, February 2007.

End Political Interference in Scientific Inquiry

Soon after taking office, the President should issue an executive order that clearly states the importance of federal climate science. The order should reinstate the principles of scientific freedom in the federal government and forbid any public official from undue interference in scientific inquiry and reporting.

The order should instruct every agency involved with climate science to establish a policy that its scientists will:

1. Have the right of final review of the technical content of federal reports
2. Be allowed free access to the media
3. Be permitted to release a scientific report to the public in draft form if an agency doesn't give the report timely approval

Appoint the Nation's Best Experts to Climate-Critical Positions in the Federal Government

The President and his Cabinet secretaries will appoint thousands of people to political positions in the administration, including many jobs that participate in or oversee federal climate policy and science. The President should direct that these jobs be filled with highly qualified professionals rather than with special-interest lobbyists.

PCAP has created an inventory of climate-critical positions in the administration and a "Who's Who in Climate Action"—a list of experts in climate science, policy, and communications the President can consider for those jobs.

During the transition period between the November 4 election and inauguration, the President's team should meet with Senate leaders to coordinate and expedite Senate confirmation of the President's climate-critical appointees.

Raise the Profile of Science in the Federal Government

The President should reestablish the position of Assistant to the President for Science and Technology as a direct report to the chief executive and should encourage Congress to fund the Office of Technology Assessment to advise lawmakers on the complex and evolving science and technology issues related to global warming.

Restore the Government's Leadership Role in Climate Science and Technology

The President should direct the administrator of NASA to restore the phrase "understand and protect the home planet" in the agency's mission statement. The restoration of that passage will help demonstrate the federal government's renewed commitment to understanding the earth's life-support systems and how to protect them.

The President should work with Congress to provide adequate funding to climate-related science. According to the National Research Council, cuts proposed by the Bush administration in the budget for earth sciences would result in "severe impacts on the long-term strategy and capacity building" in climate research. Federal scientists report there is a critical need for new satellites and terrestrial instruments to monitor climate change, more sophisticated computer programs to analyze data and predict climate impacts, and basic and applied climate research.

A particular need is more funding to better understand the regional, local, social, and economic impacts of climate change so that state and local officials can better prepare. More than 75 percent of the natural disasters worldwide are related to weather and climate; more than one-quarter of America's gross national product is vulnerable to weather-related events that affect agriculture, transportation, safety, water supplies, and public health. Local officials need the best possible information as soon as possible to cope with these challenges, some of which already have begun to occur.

To make sure this information gets to those who can use it, the President should launch a National Climate Change Preparedness project to improve communications between federal scientists and decision-makers at all levels of government and civil society. Climate Science Watch, a program of the Government Accountability Project in Washington, D.C., has developed the details of such a project.

Comply with the Provisions of the Global Change Protection Act of 1987

The Global Change Protection Act of 1987 makes the President responsible for "developing and proposing to Congress a coordinated national policy on global climate change." The Bush administration consistently ignored deadlines the Act established for reports on climate change. The President should direct agencies to fully comply with the requirements and timetables in the Act.

Expand Public-Private Partnerships for Clean Energy Technologies

The national laboratories are allowed to enter into joint research projects with private companies under Cooperative Research and Development Agreements, or CRADAs. These agreements give private companies access to the laboratories' equipment and expertise. The new administration can better publicize and promote the availability of joint research opportunities to U.S. industry and business organizations, and to companies large and small, to speed the development and deployment of new energy efficiency and renewable energy technologies.

Educate the Next Generation of U.S. Scientists

Nearly 80 percent of American adults believe science is not receiving the attention it deserves in our schools. The urgency of global climate change clearly has not created the surge of interest in science that President John F. Kennedy set off when he announced that America would go to the moon.

Yet climate change is a challenge that's here to stay. All future generations will have to understand and address it. The new President should rally the nation's educators at all levels to give new emphasis to improving science education, including the dynamics and causes of global warming. Through internship programs and curricula development, America's national laboratories should help the nation's schools improve science education and incite the interest of young people in environmental studies. Federal funding for education should support "No Child Left Inside" programs at the K–12 levels. Using his bully pulpit, the President should call on America's young people to enroll in environmental studies and professions—to enlist in an ecological army that finally resolves the longstanding conflict between economic development and environmental health.

It's not just children who need better access to climate education. Public and private officials who set local policies on land use, public health, emergency response, transportation planning, building codes, and utility management—to name just a few professions that affect or will be affected by climate change—all need a better understanding of global warming and the problems it will pose in their localities and professions. The President should tell agencies to work closely with national associations representing public officials and key professions—ranging from the U.S. Conference of Mayors to the Association of State Floodplain Managers— to provide the information they need to anticipate, prepare for, mitigate, and adapt to climate change.

6.

The Clean Energy Surge

The United States lacks a coherent national energy policy. That's a recipe for disaster in a time of growing greenhouse gas emissions, peaking oil supplies, and intensifying international competition for petroleum, natural gas, uranium, and other finite resources.

The basic elements of an effective energy policy are clear:

- Dramatically increase America's energy efficiency in every sector—vehicles, buildings, industry, power generation, and government operations
- Change the nature of our energy supplies from energy resources that are finite and carbon intensive, to resources that are domestic, renewable, and clean

Soon after taking office, the new President should launch a "clean energy surge"—a national campaign as intensive and determined as the effort Franklin Roosevelt launched, and the American people executed, to win World War II.

Why is energy efficiency the first priority? Consider this: We waste more energy in electric generation each year than Japan uses to power its entire economy! The typical coal-fired electric plant is only 30–40 percent efficient, meaning that most of the energy value of the fuel is lost. In the conventional automobile, only a small fraction of the energy it burns moves the vehicle forward. Until Congress raised the efficiency standard for cars and light trucks last December, the United States ranked last among major nations in that category. The new U.S. standard requires that new cars achieve an average of thirty-five miles per gallon by 2020, but several automakers are promising to market cars by 2010 that achieve more than one hundred miles per gallon.

Energy efficiency is the "low-hanging fruit" of our economy—the fastest, easiest, and cheapest way to reduce our energy costs, cut our foreign trade deficit, give every household and business new disposable income, take the pressure off our electric system, and cut U.S. greenhouse gas emissions. "Improving our energy efficiency means making ourselves wealthier," notes Christine Ervin, DOE's former Assistant Secretary for Energy Efficiency and Renewable Energy.

In fact, much of the cost of addressing climate change can be offset with the dollar savings achieved by improving energy efficiency in buildings, appliances, and the industrial sector, according to a study by the global consulting firm McKinsey & Co., titled "Reducing Greenhouse Gas Emissions: How Much at What Cost?" On the personal level, consider this: We can expect the price of gasoline to continue rising long-term because of increasing worldwide demand. The cost of electricity will go up, too. Analysts at the U.S. Department of Energy estimate that electric costs will go up 35 percent if the power industry is able to develop "clean coal" technology—the process of capturing coal's carbon and burying it underground. The Sierra Club predicts the increase may be as much as 90 percent. The best way to protect ourselves from those personal price shocks is to become more efficient.

In previous chapters, I've mentioned several of the steps the President should take to launch the surge: for example, faster progress on efficiency standards for appliances, a new national model building code that leads to zero-energy performance in all new buildings by 2030, and a requirement that automakers achieve an average of fifty miles per gallon by 2020 in cars and light trucks. In addition, the President should:

- Challenge the nation to meet an aggressive new national goal for energy efficiency—a 25 percent reduction in demand by 2020
- Urge Congress to pass a national requirement that renewable energy must provide 10 percent of our electricity by 2015, 30 percent by 2020, and 50 percent by midcentury
- Require the federal government to lead the way by reducing its carbon emissions 80 percent or more by 2050
- Urge Congress to appropriate substantial new funding to help states and localities launch their own clean energy surges
- Work with Congress on a major overhaul of the federal transportation program to switch its emphasis from building more roads to helping communities create low-carbon mobility options

A few of these goals deserve more explanation.

States and Communities

When federal policy makers look at the role government can play in the transformation to a green economy, they come to an interesting realization: Much of the authority to reduce greenhouse gas emissions resides not in Washington, D.C., but in state capitols and in city halls. States are in charge of regulating utilities and establishing building codes; localities are in charge of enforcing building codes and guiding urban development. Communities decide whether to invest in mass transit, walking and bicycling paths, and high-occupancy vehicle lanes. In other words, state and local officials have the authority to make major changes in the three biggest sources of U.S. carbon emissions—electric generation, construction, and transportation.

And that's the way most state and local leaders like it. Many of them are concerned that given the urgent need to reduce emissions and increase America's energy security, Congress may preempt state and local authority, deciding that the federal government should regulate utilities and building standards, for example. But states and communities serve a vital role as laboratories of change in the United States. They are more directly accountable to local citizens. They can design programs and policies that are better suited to local conditions than a one-size-fits-all national approach.

While some nationwide standards clearly are in the national interest, and some nationwide uniformity is important so that industry doesn't have to contend with a patchwork of regulations, the federal government's role generally should be to set goals, establish minimum standards, and encourage states and cities to exceed them. The government also should provide funding, technical help, and information, which is especially important because our knowledge about climate change and its impacts is still evolving.

During the transition, the President-elect should create a task force of leading governors and mayors to frame an intergovernmental climate action plan that coordinates the powers of federal, state, and local governments. In addition, the President should join mayors and governors in encouraging Congress to provide substantial new funding for states and communities to help lead America's economic transformation. For example, the Energy Independence and Security Act that Congress passed in December 2007 created an energy efficiency block grant program that would provide $2 billion a year for five years to the nation's communities. But Congress has not yet provided the money, and it should.

In addition, Congress should appropriate $1 billion annually to the U.S. Department of Energy's State Energy Program. (President Bush proposed $50 million in his 2009 budget request.) Through that program, the Department of Energy provides grants to support energy offices and energy initiatives in each state. Congress should establish new rules for these grants. States would qualify by creating their own energy and climate security plans, tailored to their resources, politics, and energy profiles. DOE would approve each state's plan and review progress every three years to renew the state's eligibility. The new rules would encourage states to adopt portfolios of progressive energy policies; the more aggressive its plan, the more funding each state would receive. The policies the State Energy Program would support include:

- **Utility rate de-coupling**: A policy that allows utilities to earn reasonable financial returns not just from selling energy, but also from helping their customers save energy
- **Distributed generation**: The production of electricity close to where it is used (such as with rooftop solar collectors), reducing pressure on the electric distribution system and reducing the need for new transmission lines
- **Co-generation**: The practice of capturing and using waste heat from electric turbines operated by an industry or institution, resulting in much more energy production from each unit of fuel
- **Interconnection standards**: Clear and fair rules that allow utility customers to produce power while connected to the transmission grid
- **Feed-in tariffs**: Policies that guarantee customers a premium price from their utilities when they generate their own energy
- **"Smart grid" development**: State-of-the-art transmission systems that reduce power interruptions, provide new opportunities

for customers to save energy, and make it easier to move renewable power around the country

- **Capturing stranded renewable resources:** Extending transmission lines to areas with good wind, solar, or geothermal resources to move the electricity to customers
- **Renewable energy portfolio standards:** Requirements that utilities generate a percentage of their electricity from solar, wind, or other renewable resources*

Appliance Efficiency Standards

Appliances use 20 percent of the energy consumed in a typical household. The Energy Information Administration says that new appliances will be one of the major causes of higher greenhouse gas emissions in the United States between now and 2030. The good news is that the Energy Independence and Security Act (EISA) of 2007 sets new statutory efficiency standards for residential clothes washers, dishwashers, refrigerators, and many other items.

The bad news is that the Department of Energy, which is responsible for working with industry to establish standards for other types of appliances and equipment, is years behind schedule. The next Secretary of Energy should act quickly to identify and propose solutions to the department's logjam. In the meantime, Congress should allow states to set their own standards for appliances when DOE fails to do so on time.

Investing in New Technology

To achieve the level of energy and climate security we need to sustain the American Dream, the clean energy surge can't be a one-

---

* For reports on which states already have instituted these and other progressive energy policies, see the Environmental Protection Agency's Web site.

time thing. We will need a continuous flow of innovation and new technologies to repower every sector of the economy, including factories, farms, and individual households.

We'll need to maintain our entrepreneurial edge, too, to compete in the huge emerging global marketplace for clean energy. We need a long-term commitment and plan for developing new technologies and moving them rapidly from laboratory to market.

Today, we are greatly under-investing in energy research, particularly at a time we need game-changing breakthroughs in carbon-free energy resources and products. University of California, Berkeley energy experts Daniel Kammen and Gregory Nemet report that energy research and development (R&D) spending by U.S. companies dropped 50 percent between 1991 and 2003. They calculate that the federal investment in energy R&D should increase as much as tenfold, to $30 billion yearly, if we wish to hold carbon dioxide levels at double preindustrial levels.

We should encourage innovation outside the laboratory, too. The next great invention may be discovered in a garage, in the back room of a small business, or in a college dormitory, as has been the case in some of the most significant advances in the information technology revolution.

History offers an example of one creative approach to spurring innovation. In 1987, the international community agreed to reduce the use of chlorofluorocarbons (CFCs) used in refrigeration and foaming agents. The chemicals were causing a hole in the earth's ozone layer. The protocol caused a great deal of uncertainty among appliance manufacturers, however, who were not sure how to replace their old refrigerants.

In response, the U.S. Environmental Protection Agency joined a nonprofit consortium that offered a "Golden Carrot Award"— a prize of $30 million contributed by a number of appliance companies—to the manufacturer that developed the most energy-efficient, CFC-free refrigerator. The new refrigerator had to be at least 25 percent more efficient than the federal government's standard at the time. In addition, the rules of the contest stipulated that the winning manufacturer had to produce and distribute 250,000 of the new refrigerators between 1994 and 1997.

The winner was Whirlpool. It produced a refrigerator that was 40 percent more efficient than the 1993 federal standard, that cost the same as a conventional model, that would save customers up to six hundred dollars over its lifetime, and that was expected to reduce power plant carbon dioxide emissions by 7.5 million tons every decade. The contest revolutionized the refrigerator industry.

Similar prizes should now be offered for breakthroughs that help us build the new energy economy. To cite just a few examples, we need better ways to store solar energy when the sun is shining and wind energy when the wind is blowing, improved battery technologies for electric vehicles, and rapid advances in making transportation fuels from organic wastes and nonfood farm crops.

In the Energy Independence and Security Act of 2007, Congress authorized $1 billion over ten years for the Department of Energy for "H-Prizes" to spur the development of technologies that utilize hydrogen. But we need a much wider range of breakthroughs. As I mentioned in Chapter 2, PCAP proposes that Congress allocate $1 billion for "platinum carrot awards" to innovators who develop other transformative energy technologies over the next five years.

7.

Green for All: Equity and Opportunity

Our job as a nation is to implement a national energy policy that replaces our current recipe for disaster with a recipe for prosperity. But we have another job, too, because there's no getting around the downside of this kind of sweeping change: The transition to a new postcarbon economy will cause hardship and dislocation for some families, businesses, and communities.

- If Congress puts a price on carbon—the best way to get the marketplace involved in cutting greenhouse gas emissions— consumers will have to pay more for natural gas, coal, gasoline, and oil.
- If we begin a deliberate effort—as we must—to move away from conventional coal-fired electricity and petroleum, then miners and drillers will lose jobs, and communities in coal and oil country will lose their tax base.
- If U.S. companies pay more money for fossil energy while companies in other countries do not, our industries will be less able to compete globally.

So the next question is this: How do we make sure that America's energy revolution is equitable and that no one is left behind?

Every new technology causes dislocation for those whose livelihood depended on the old order. Blacksmiths and farriers lost jobs when automobiles replaced horses. Typewriter-makers lost jobs when personal computers replaced Smith Coronas. Today, workers in U.S. car companies are losing jobs because the Big Three failed to anticipate that rising oil prices would create demand for hybrid vehicles rather than SUVs. The evolution of technology has always forced some workers to find new trades and some communities to find a new tax base. But overall, the evolution of technology has been good for the American economy.

In 2002, the Economic Policy Institute (EPI) published a package of policy proposals that it said would develop new energy efficiency and renewable energy technologies, reduce U.S. greenhouse gas emissions by 50 percent, create 1.4 million jobs, eliminate oil imports from OPEC, and save money for every American household, all by 2020. At the same time, however, those achievements would result in layoffs in the coal, utility, and rail transportation businesses.

Government policies and programs can, and should, ease the pain of those who are dislocated in the transition. We should also make sure that both the costs and benefits of climate action are distributed as equitably as possible. One way or another, a historic transition is underway. If we try to prolong the status quo, we will become a nation plagued by catastrophic climate change. The impacts of global warming, some of them already being felt in the United States, will harm public health and safety, subject people to extreme weather and natural disasters, bring drought and fire, disrupt agriculture, and result in the loss of coastal areas where much of our population lives. The cost of doing nothing about climate change would be far, far higher than the cost of dealing with it. Unless we rise to its challenge, global warming will cause traumas that make the dislocations of deliberate economic transformation look like a minor inconvenience.

On the other hand, as I detailed in Chapter 2, affirmative climate action will produce millions of new jobs, stop the torrent of energy dollars flooding out of our economy, help us avoid oil wars, and end the pain of volatile energy prices. Over the past five years, our dependence on oil has cost the U.S. economy $1.7 trillion, including $1 trillion transferred to oil-producing nations. Think for a moment of the differences between today's oil-shocked economy, and a new twenty-first century economy powered by domestic solar power, wind, and other renewable resources that are low cost, pollution free, and limitless.

The following are just a few ideas about how to help those least able to cope with the changes that must come.

Families

Families will need help coping with higher energy prices, whether they are caused by the world economy, climate policy, or both. Funding for these solutions can be found in the new revenues the federal government would earn in a cap-and-trade system.

As I described in Chapter 4, those revenues are expected to total between $100 billion and $200 billion the first year the system is in operation. By midcentury, the system could result in more than $6 trillion in new government revenue.*

Peter Barnes of the Tomales Bay Institute proposes that all of these revenues be returned as equal monthly dividends to every American. Barnes and many other supporters of this idea believe

---

* This estimate is based on the cap-and-trade bill that progressed farthest in Congress so far—the Warner-Lieberman bill introduced in the 110th Congress.

it would reinforce the idea that the atmosphere belongs to us all; we all suffer from its degradation, and we all should benefit from its protection.

Others believe that the revenues, or some portion of them, should be reserved for lower-income families. The Center on Budget and Policy Priorities has calculated that just 14 percent of the value of emissions allowances under a cap-and-trade system would be sufficient to protect the poorest fifth of U.S. households from higher energy prices and to partially offset the costs for those with "modestly higher incomes."

The Presidential Climate Action Plan advocates a hybrid of these ideas—a cap-and-invest arrangement in which one-third of auction revenues are returned in the form of annual dividends or tax benefits for American families. One-third of the revenues would be used to address the equity issues discussed in this chapter and to help families, communities, and businesses adapt to climate change. The last third would be used to dramatically increase the federal investment in clean energy technologies. Over time, as the new energy economy takes hold, PCAP recommends that all of the revenues be returned to the American people in annual dividends or tax benefits.

In the meantime, the President should propose more funding for the federal programs that already are in place to help the elderly and low-income families cope with and avoid energy emergencies. The Low Income Home Energy Assistance Program (LIHEAP) operated by the Department of Health and Human Services helps pay fuel bills for families threatened with having their heat cut off in the winter. The Weatherization Assistance Program (WAP) administered by the Department of Energy hires local crews to insulate, weather-strip, and make other important improvements to the houses of low-income individuals and families. In other words,

WAP makes permanent efficiency improvements that prevent the energy emergencies that LIHEAP addresses, and creates local jobs in the process. So far, WAP has helped weatherize only 5 million of the nation's 28 million eligible homes.

The Department of Energy's Web site says that President George W. Bush "designated weatherization as a priority for his administration and committed DOE to request funding increases of $1.4 billion over the next ten years." But the Bush administration's 2009 budget proposed that the Weatherization Assistance Program be killed, with no funding at all. In the same budget, the administration proposed a 22 percent cut in funding for LIHEAP, meaning that more than 1 million fewer low-income and elderly families would receive emergency fuel assistance.

The next President will present his 2009 budget to Congress just weeks after taking office. He should propose that WAP receive $1.4 billion a year (up from $227 million in 2008) and that LIHEAP be fully funded at its 2008 level.

Workers

In its 2002 report, the Economic Policy Institute proposed that the federal government provide the following help to workers displaced by economic transformation:

- Every worker who loses his or her job in an energy-producing or energy-intensive industry would receive compensation equal to two years of full income, including health and retirement benefits.
- Affected workers should be provided up to four years of college education or other professional training.
- Older workers should be provided the option of benefits that create a bridge to retirement.

North Arkansas College
1515 Pioneer Drive
Harrison, AR 72601

The transition to a green economy will open new career paths not only for displaced workers, but also for those who are jobless now and have limited opportunities. Activist Majora Carter, founder of Sustainable South Bronx, is demonstrating how a poor urban neighborhood, where local officials had dumped wastes and located polluting industries, can pull itself up by the bootstraps by "greening" itself. Carter and Van Jones of the Ella Baker Center for Human Rights in Oakland, California, led the charge for congressional approval of a Green Jobs Act that authorizes $125 million to train thirty thousand young people in "green collar jobs"—for example, home weatherization and the installation of solar panels and wind-energy systems. While the green economy will produce jobs at all income levels, many will go to at-risk youths and jobless adults who are now taking their first steps onto the career paths of the future.

In addition to the jobs created by the Green Jobs Act, the President should propose the creation of a volunteer Green Job Corps under the umbrella of the AmeriCorps program. The corps would be open to the 1.5 million Americans between the ages of eighteen and twenty-four who are neither employed nor in school. Corps members could help communities with climate adaptation and mitigation projects, including wetland and watershed restoration for flood prevention, reforestation of areas where trees have been destroyed by pests or fire, and the development of natural corridors through urban areas to help wildlife move northward as their old habitats become warmer. Participants would be paid a stipend, plus five thousand dollars for each year of service, which would help program graduates go to college, buy their first home, or start a business.

History again provides a model—the Civilian Conservation Corps created under President Franklin Roosevelt in 1933 to help reduce unemployment caused by the Depression.

Communities

The federal government operates a number of programs to spur job creation and economic development in depressed areas. Where the law gives the administration discretion in how these programs are prioritized, the President should direct agencies to target the communities most severely affected by climate change, climate policy, and economic transformation—including the mining and drilling communities I mentioned earlier.

One such program is the Empowerment Zone/Enterprise Communities initiative started during the Clinton administration to provide an economic spark in the nation's poorest urban neighborhoods and rural areas. The President should direct the Department of Agriculture and the Department of Housing and Urban Development to identify "Climate Enterprise Zones" where federal and state incentives are used to attract new "green" industrial development, such as manufacturing and assembly plants for solar and wind energy systems.

Industries

What would happen if the big industries of the fossil energy era became allies rather than obstacles, and winners rather than losers, in the economic transformation? What if oil companies began investing some of their record profits in a sustainable energy future? What if the tax breaks we give oil and gas companies to "drill, baby, drill" were used instead to help them develop wind, solar, geothermal, hydroelectric, and bio-energy?

That future might not be so far away. Some of the energy giants' stockholders apparently can see a time down the road when oil rigs go the way of buggy whips. As the *International Herald Tribune* reported in May 2008:

Exxon Mobil posted the two most profitable years on record in 2007 and 2008 but instead of warm applause at this year's annual meeting, the company's officers had to contend with calls for change due to its lack of spending on green energy sources.

The Rockefeller family, descendants of John D. Rockefeller, who founded Exxon precursor Standard Oil, publicly backed a number of shareholder resolutions, including one advocating the split of Exxon's chairman and chief executive positions, because of the company's slight investment in green energy sources. . . .

Other oil companies, including Royal Dutch Shell and BP, already have renewable energy operations. Still, even they are being pushed to do more by investors attending their annual meetings this year who called on them to boost their investments, which currently amount to 1 percent of total capital expenditure.

With oil prices soaring to records of more than $130 a barrel, the firms certainly have plenty of money to invest. But instead of splurging on research on new forms of energy, they are returning billions of dollars of excess cash to investors in the form of share buybacks, which help support the stock price, and dividends.

The paper quotes innovation expert Steve Wunker of the consulting firm Innosight: "Most oil firms seem profoundly uninterested in disrupting a business model that is delivering substantial returns." Of course, that's what the Big Three automakers thought when they bet on their more profitable sport-utility vehicles.

If we continue offering public subsidies to fossil energy industries, they should not be to produce more oil, coal, and gas, but to begin evolving into industries that power the new economy. Any such subsidies—investment tax credits for example—should be designed to leverage large investments by those companies of their own capital. One model is Barack Obama's proposal to help the U.S. auto industry make the transition to plug-in hybrid and other low-carbon vehicles.

And what of the concern that if America cracks down on carbon emissions, our companies won't be able to compete with countries where fossil energy remains cheap and greenhouse gas emissions unaddressed? One solution is a "border adjustment"—a fee placed on products that come from countries that have not put a price on carbon.

The point is, we can help those least able to cope with the changes ahead, and we should.

8.

Citizenship and Stewardship

In a letter to James Madison in 1789, Thomas Jefferson stated that each generation has an obligation to pass the earth along to the next generation free of "debts and incumbrances [*sic*]." Otherwise, he wrote, "the earth would belong to the dead and not to the living."

Jefferson was referring to financial debt. But today, we must understand these rights and obligations in the context of the climate issues facing our generation, including the fact that we are causing irreparable harm to our planet and all of the creatures that inhabit it, including ourselves.

The Founders could not have anticipated that human affairs would reach a point at which life, liberty, and the pursuit of happiness would be threatened by global environmental degradation. Even if we, like Jefferson, think about intergenerational responsibility in fiscal terms, we understand better now that natural resources are a form of capital and that ecosystems perform services of enormous economic value to human societies—$33 trillion a year worldwide, by one estimate.

The depletion of natural capital—whether animal species, forests, fresh water, fertile soil, the oceans, or the atmosphere—undermines our wealth and that of future generations. The carbon dioxide emissions that are causing atmospheric warming persist for hundreds, even thousands, of years. It is a debt that our generation is leaving for many generations to follow.

That brings us to the principle of stewardship. A steward is someone who manages another's property. In the environmental context, it is the practice of managing the earth's natural resources on behalf of all of us who depend upon them for health and prosperity, now and in the future. Every president in modern times has recognized that protection of natural resources is a vital responsibility for us all. In 2006, for example, former President Bill Clinton said, "There has never been a nation destroyed by terrorism alone and it's not about to start now. But I think this climate change has the capacity to change the way all of us live on Earth."

Many religions also recognize the idea that stewardship is the obligation of humankind to care for God's creation. For example, the stewardship ethic was behind the Vatican's declaration early in 2008 that ecological offenses are a modern evil. Pope Benedict has issued a series of appeals for the protection of the environment, noting that issues such as global warming have become gravely important for the entire human race. His predecessor, Pope John Paul II, signed a declaration in 2002 that as the world faces an environmental crisis, Christians have a responsibility to combat it and need to develop an "environmental ethos."

The principle of stewardship also appears in national law. When it passed the National Environmental Policy Act (NEPA) in 1969, for example, Congress required federal officials to consider the environmental impacts of their decisions. The purpose of the law is to "encourage productive and enjoyable harmony between man and his environment; to promote efforts which will prevent or eliminate damage to the environment and biosphere and stimulate the health and welfare of man. . . ." Further, NEPA declares, it is "the continuing responsibility of the Federal Government to use all practicable means, consistent with other essential considerations of national policy, to fulfill the responsibilities of each generation as trustee of the environment for succeeding generations." NEPA remains the law of the land today.

At the University of Oregon School of Law, Professor Mary Christina Wood is laying the groundwork for litigation to establish the legal principle that the atmosphere is a public trust—an asset owned by us all—and that government officials at all levels have a responsibility to protect it on our behalf. "Our new leaders can and must reframe government's *discretion* to destroy Nature into an *obligation* to protect Nature and to ensure Natural Resource Stewardship," she writes. At the University of Vermont, scholars are engaged in an analysis of whether each generation of Americans has an enforceable legal obligation to future generations.

Internationally, the United States is one of nearly 200 nations that have agreed to the United Nations Framework Convention on Climate Change, signed by President George H. W. Bush in 1992. While the agreement is nonbinding, signatories promised to "protect the climate system for present and future generations."

Clearly, an environmental crisis that threatens the earth's life-support systems undermines our rights to life and the pursuit of happiness. What about liberty? The National Intelligence Council, in a classified assessment in June 2008, determined that climate change is a threat to national security. That finding confirmed conclusions by a number of military and civilian defense experts who now regard global warming as a "threat multiplier" that will cause turmoil in some of the most volatile regions of the world. Turmoil, they have concluded, creates fertile ground for terrorist organizations to recruit new members. Military experts also agree that resource conflicts will increase as the rapidly growing world population competes for limited resources such as oil, gas, and minerals.

Since the attacks on the Pentagon and World Trade Center, we have seen an erosion of liberty, ranging from the frustrating and increasingly intrusive security checks at the nation's airports to the rollback of our constitutional rights to privacy and due process. In short, when fossil energy consumption causes greenhouse gas emissions, and greenhouse gas emissions cause climate change, and climate change threatens our national security, and our response erodes our freedoms, then we must conclude that the carbon economy undermines our right to liberty.

What natural capital is at stake if climate change continues unabated and we do not take on our stewardship responsibilities for the environment? The Intergovernmental Panel on Climate Change (IPCC) has concluded that the "resilience of many ecosystems is likely to be exceeded this century by an unprecedented combination of climate change, associated disturbances (e.g., flooding, drought, wildfire, insects, ocean acidification), and other global change drivers (e.g., land-use change, pollution)."

The "Millennium Ecosystem Assessment," a study conducted between 2001 and 2005 by 1,300 experts from ninety-five countries, concluded that 60 percent of the ecosystem services that support life on earth are being degraded. "Over the past fifty years, humans have changed ecosystems more rapidly and extensively than in any comparable period of time in human history, largely to meet rapidly growing demands for food, fresh water, timber, fiber, and fuel," the experts reported. "This has resulted in a substantially and largely irreversible loss in the diversity of life on Earth."

The IPCC estimates that 20–30 percent of the plant and animal species that scientists have studied so far are at risk of extinction if the atmosphere grows 1.5–2.5 degrees centigrade warmer—which is likely at current rates of greenhouse gas emissions. Dr. Peter Raven, director of the Missouri Botanical Gardens, projects that if the present rate of habitat loss continues, that factor alone is likely to cause the annual extinction of fifteen thousand species.*

In human terms, forests that we depend upon for lumber are threatened by pests and fire; wildlife we depend upon for hunting and fishing are among the threatened species; farmland we depend upon for food and fiber is threatened by drought; animal and plant species we depend upon for new medicines are threatened by the cutting of rain forests; oceans that we depend upon for food and recreation are threatened by rising temperatures.

The following are some of the actions the next President should take to make stewardship a stronger principle in national policy:

1. **Issue a directive that federal employees must regard the atmosphere as a public trust and protect it as such.** Incorporate this responsibility in federal job descriptions and employee performance reviews that are the basis for salary bonuses and promotions.

2. **Require climate impact statements for all federally funded projects.** Include climate impact assessments in the requirements of the National Environmental Policy Act. In addition, direct that all agencies must include climate

---

* For a much more complete description of the impacts of climate change on ecosystems, see http://www.climateactionproject.com/docs/white_papers/9_Natural _Resources_Extended_12.11.07.pdf.

impact statements in their budget proposals in reports to Congress and the American public.

3. **Develop a system to regularly measure national progress on stewardship.** Direct the Council on Environmental Quality to expedite the development of national sustainability indicators that assess the condition of the nation's natural resources and measure America's progress on reducing the ecological impacts of climate change.

4. **Improve ecosystem management.** Direct federal agencies to assess the key ecological services and systems expected to be adversely affected by climate change and to develop management plans consistent with those impacts.

5. **Identify and fully fund critical stewardship programs.** Identify federal programs that are important to the health of soils, forests, watersheds, and other critical assets and work with Congress to ensure that these programs are adequately funded.

6. **Strengthen our forests.** Due in part to warmer winters and drought, millions of acres of pine forest are being destroyed by bark beetles in the United States. Direct the Departments of Agriculture and Interior to identify climate-tolerant species for forestation and reforestation programs.

7. **Develop "ark" projects and wildlife corridors.** As the climate warms, plant and animals species will attempt to adapt by moving northward, following the temperatures to which they are best suited. In some cases, urban development will get in the way of migration. Direct the Department of Interior to develop guidelines for cities to create natural corridors that accommodate migration. Direct the Interior Department to develop guidelines for the creation of "ark" projects to preserve species threatened by habitat loss.

8. **Conserve existing forests and land for carbon sequestration.** Among other services, privately owned forests provide wildlife habitat and carbon sequestration. Direct the U.S. Department of Agriculture to propose improvements in federal incentives to keep forested land forested and marginal land out of production to enhance carbon sequestration despite increasing pressures to expand cropland for energy production.

9. **Convene a White House conference on ecological literacy.** Bring the nation's leading educators and ecologists to the White House to propose improvements in America's ecological education at all grade levels. Include adult education programs for those entering climate-related professions and for public policy makers.

Don't Forget Water

The availability of fresh water has been called "the next big crisis" in the United States and worldwide. About one-fifth of the world's population—1.2 billion people—lacks adequate supplies of potable water. Here at home, the American West is experiencing both population growth and drought, putting cities in competition with agriculture and energy production for water supplies.

The predicted shortages of water in some areas of the United States require a comprehensive strategy for water management and conservation, adapted to regional needs. Aggressive water conservation programs and watershed management and restoration programs (including wetland restoration) must be part of this mix. The 44th President should do the following:

- Direct the Department of Energy to give highest priority to the development, demonstration, and deployment of fuels and energy technologies that minimize water use while reducing CO_2 emissions

- Direct the General Services Administration to utilize water-saving designs in federal construction and instruct agencies to reward similar designs in state, local, and private developments that receive federal funding
- Convene a high-profile summit of national stakeholders in water management to frame a national water resources conservation strategy covering potable and irrigation water, and the preservation and restoration of wetlands and riparian (river) areas
- Order the Department of Agriculture to redouble its effort to help farmers adopt water-saving techniques for crop irrigation, ranging from prompt repair of leaks to precision irrigation systems and drought-tolerant crops
- Request the Environmental Protection Agency to increase its effort to encourage energy and resource efficiency in municipal water consumption and treatment

In addition, the President should propose the following actions by Congress:

- Establish a national competitive grants program, open to states and local governments, to analyze water conservation and water supply system operational changes needed to increase the resilience of public water supply systems
- Revise federal water and sewer infrastructure funding to give priority to those projects that achieve the highest practical levels of water conservation
- Phase out federal irrigation subsidies that promote unsustainable water use, particularly in the western United States

- Require the U.S. Army Corps of Engineers to give priority to projects that protect public safety and restore critical degraded coastal and river ecosystems

When the first members of the baby boom generation were born sixty years ago, the world population was 2.3 billion. It took more than ten thousand generations to reach that point. Then, within one lifetime, the population nearly tripled to its current level—6.5 billion. By midcentury, the 9 billion people expected to inhabit the earth—each of them—will be entitled to the inalienable rights of life, liberty, and the pursuit of happiness. If the world's people continue believing that those rights can only be obtained with large carbon footprints—if stewardship does not become the guiding ethic of economic and human development—we will not only mortgage the future. We will bankrupt it.

9.

Adaptation Versus Mitigation: Why Not Both?

As we've seen, we must "mitigate" global warming by rapidly and dramatically cutting our greenhouse gas emissions. But what about the climate changes that are already underway and certain to become more severe in the years ahead?

The hard reality is this: With the greenhouse gases we have emitted in the past, we're already committed to painful and costly consequences for many years to come. As I've written, a growing number of scientists are concluding that climate change has already begun in the United States in the form of extreme weather, flooding, drought, and wildfire. If those problems aren't personal enough, allergies and hay fever are growing more widespread and severe due to longer pollen seasons resulting from climate change. For this reason the national campaign against climate change must include adaptation as well as mitigation.

Adaptation takes many forms. In coastal areas, it includes such measures as restoring wetlands and other natural features that reduce storm surges and designing buildings capable of tolerating hurricane-force winds. It includes restoring the natural flood-control features of rivers and watersheds. It also involves more stringent restrictions against building in floodplains, and more projects to relocate residents who already live in harm's way.

In agriculture, it means growing more drought-tolerant crops, using water more efficiently, and guarding against new types of pests. In forested areas, it means protecting buildings against wildfires and combating forest-destroying insects. In communities, it means better preparations for natural disasters, heat waves, and other public health emergencies.

Adaptation will cost money, but it will cost much less than the damage to crops, buildings, cities, infrastructure, and public health that will occur without adequate preparation. Much of this work and investment will have to take place locally, but the federal government can help in several ways.

Create New Designs for the Built Environment

The President should direct a variety of federal agencies—the Departments of Energy, Homeland Security, Transportation, Housing and Urban Development, and Interior, for example—to develop new standards and guidelines for incorporating adaptation into buildings, urban infrastructure, coastal and watershed management, and so on. In Chapter 2, I talked about the enormous investment America must make to repair and modernize its critical infrastructure. No water system, road, bridge, levee, building, utility grid, or mass transit facility should be built in the United States without being designed for adaptation—and without using the most climate-friendly materials available.

Direct the Federal Climate Change Science Program to Develop Better Information on Local Climate Impacts

After auditing the government's Climate Change Science Program in 2007, the National Research Council reported that too little research has been done on the regional, local, social, and economic impacts of climate change. As I touched upon in Chapter 5, this information is vital to local officials, health professionals, and others to help them understand and adapt to the impact of global warming. Federal scientists need adequate funding for satellite capabilities that allow them to study climate change. If necessary, the government should reduce funding for President Bush's Mission to Mars program until we better understand our mission on earth.

Urge Locals to Take the No-Regrets Approach

Using his bully pulpit, the President should encourage state and local leaders to adopt a "no-regrets" adaptation strategy. That means investing in sound adaptation measures even if local leaders and voters are unsure how severe the climate change will be—and even if, despite all evidence to the contrary, they doubt that climate change is real.

Many of the things we need to do to adjust to climate impacts are beneficial anyway—for example, weatherizing buildings to make them more comfortable during heat waves, building better protection against destructive weather, or improving public health emergency preparedness. At the same time, local officials should adopt a "do no harm" approach by promising not to increase the danger for other communities. Some local flood control measures, for example, actually make flooding worse for communities up- or downriver.

Make Sure the Feds Are Better Prepared

This is the "No More Katrinas" plan. For any number of reasons, FEMA has performed poorly since it was transferred to the Department of Homeland Security. We can expect more severe damage from natural disasters as climate change gets worse. The federal government must be prepared to more rapidly deploy water, power systems, medical supplies, and other essentials. There should be fewer bureaucratic layers between the director of FEMA and the White House. The President should propose to Congress that FEMA be made an independent agency once again.

In the meantime, the President should order his FEMA director to collaborate with organizations such as the National Emergency Management Association and the Association of State Floodplain Managers to determine what changes are needed in the nation's disaster preparation, prevention, and response programs. For example, as the weather changes, we have to update maps of floodways, floodplains, and coastal hazard areas, and we have to adjust rules about whether to allow people to build and rebuild in those areas.

In addition, FEMA should begin working closely with federal, state, and local agencies that are expert in natural resource management. If we had studied natural systems more closely in the past, we might have known not to destroy the coastal wetlands that once served as a shock absorber against storm surges in New Orleans, or the meanders that retarded flooding along rivers in the Midwest. It's time for us to make natural systems our allies, rather than jumping to the conclusion that we can or should attempt to control them with manmade structures. Some call this new approach eco-engineering. I call it engineering with humility.

Watch Out for Taxpayer Exposure

The federal government operates two hazard insurance programs because the private sector won't. FEMA administers the National Flood Insurance Program (NFIP); the U.S. Department of Agriculture is in charge of the Federal Crop Insurance Program (FCIP). Both are in trouble. Between 1980 and 2005, the NFIP's exposure quadrupled, nearing $1 trillion. The program borrowed more than $17 billion from the U.S. Treasury to pay claims following Katrina, Rita, and Wilma. It has been unable to repay this debt, so taxpayers will likely foot the bill.

Since 1980, taxpayer exposure under FCIP has increased twenty-six-fold to $44 billion. The demands on both programs will increase, perhaps dramatically, because of climate change. The President should ask FEMA and the USDA to assess the viability of these two programs based on current science and recommend reforms that will lead to less taxpayer exposure. We must start asking hard questions—for example, about whether any government insurance or other assistance should be given to a home or business owner who, after losses following one natural disaster chooses to return to a hazard area to risk the same losses again. And we should ask whether taxpayers should be expected to help any developer or property owner who knowingly builds in a floodplain.

Deploy a Green Citizens' Army

In Chapter 7, I talked about creating a new Green Jobs Corps designed to get 1.5 million American youth onto green career paths. One important mission of the corps should be to train these young people in the skills we need for climate mitigation and adaptation and then send them to the communities that most need their help.

Create a "Green Room"

When the Clinton administration launched its collection of climate-action initiatives, it created a "Green Room" in the basement of the Department of Energy's headquarters in Washington, D.C. The room was staffed by experts from federal agencies, assigned to make it a one-stop shop of information on climate action. The Green Room was closed when the Clinton team left office. It's time to hook up the telephones and computers again.

Agency experts who are able to provide the best available information about climate mitigation and adaptation, including information about federal programs, should be available on the Web and by phone to state and local officials, health providers, business leaders—anyone who's ready to join the national campaign against climate change.

10.

Redefining National Security

If we learned that al Qaeda was secretly developing a new terrorist technique that could disrupt water supplies around the globe, force tens of millions from their homes, and potentially endanger our entire planet, we would be aroused into a frenzy and deploy every possible asset to neutralize the threat. Yet that is precisely the threat that we're creating ourselves with our greenhouse gases.

—Nicholas D. Kristof, *The New York Times* (August 16, 2007)

As we've heard from the nation's military experts, global climate change is not just an environmental issue anymore. In one recent report, eleven retired U.S. generals and admirals brought together by the Center for Naval Analysis in Washington, D.C., concluded that it must be dealt with now. Not tomorrow. *Now.*

It is time, too, to confront the closely related national security threat of oil. Its carbon emissions greatly exacerbate climate change, while our dependence on imports increases our vulnerability in a multitude of ways.

First, many of the experts who now recognize the security implications of global warming also acknowledge the growing likelihood of "resource conflicts" as more nations compete for a finite—and soon a declining—supply of oil. The U.S. Department of Energy funded a study in 2005 of what might happen when world oil production peaks, a milestone that some say has already occurred. The authors conclude: "The peaking of world oil production presents the U.S. and the world with an unprecedented risk management problem. As peaking is approached, liquid fuel prices and price volatility will increase dramatically, and, without timely mitigation, the economic, social, and political costs will be unprecedented."

Second, as we should have learned from the Arab oil embargoes in the 1970s, our economy is frightfully vulnerable to supply disruptions from producing nations. The United States imports more than 60 percent of its oil today, more than twice the level of imports during the embargoes. The U.S. Energy Information Administration predicts we will import nearly 70 percent of our oil by 2030. About 40 percent of our imports come from members of the Organization of Petroleum Exporting Countries (OPEC)—the group of producers that collude on global oil supplies and prices. Some part of the $1 trillion in American wealth we transferred to oil-producing nations over the past five years has gone to countries that sponsor terrorist organizations. In other words, some part of each tank of gasoline we buy finances terrorism.

Third, our thirst for oil poisons our foreign policy and subverts our aspiration to see democracy spread around the world. In 2006, after sponsoring a series of roundtables attended by an array of specialists, the Aspen Institute issued a summary of the discussion with this assessment: "Many countries that are rich in energy resources are prone to corruption, are autocratic and repress political dissent in the name of stability. If the United States associates with these countries to obtain energy supplies, it risks alienating the oppressed population and undermining its credibility on other foreign policy goals, such as the promotion of democracy and human rights."

"Oil is now the centerpiece of America's foreign policy, economic policy, defense policy, environmental policy, and energy policy," says former Senator Gary Hart. "So long as the economy of the United States is held hostage by foreign oil producers, America will remain vulnerable to volatile prices, supply interruptions, the overthrow of producing governments, and regional unrest, instability, and conflict."

One of the big lessons we should learn from the home mortgage crisis and meltdown on Wall Street is that we must do a far better job anticipating crises before they overwhelm us. Oil supply and climate change are two such issues, the twin, interrelated security threats of our time that need to be addressed now. We recommend that the new President implement the actions outlined below.

Create an OPEC for Importing Nations

One of the challenges of energy security is that petroleum is a global commodity in a global market operating within a global economy. In other words, every nation is connected to every other. The United States could stop importing petroleum tomorrow and our economy still would be vulnerable to oil shocks. For example, half of our top ten trading partners are net oil importers, including China and Japan. If they have an oil crisis, we also will feel the pain.

Since global problems require global solutions, the President should propose that oil-importing nations join the United States to create an Organization of Petroleum Importing Countries (OPIC).

Members would collaborate on research, best practices, and policies to reduce their reliance on oil imports and eventually, for the sake of climate stability, their dependence on oil from all sources.

Review the Persian Gulf Police Force

The Persian Gulf region is the world's largest single source of oil. By one estimate, U.S. taxpayers spend about $30 billion every year to police the region so that oil keeps flowing to the world market. The President should direct the Department of Defense to assess how well other oil-importing nations are sharing this burden with the United States and, if justified, seek additional international support.

Identify Energy Options That Solve Multiple Problems

From this point forward, the federal government should invest taxpayers' money only in energy resources and technologies that address energy and climate security at the same time. We need to engage in problem solving, not problem switching. For example, the coal industry would like to make liquid fuel from coal and the petroleum industry would like to produce oil from shale, both to reduce oil imports. But those new fuels would result in much higher carbon emissions, not to mention great amounts of water consumption and other environmental costs. Likewise, making ethanol from corn reduces oil consumption, but it is energy- and water-intensive and competes with food production.

The President should direct the Secretary of Energy to develop a registry of fuels and energy technologies that produce the most important benefits with the least cost, improve our national security as well as our emissions profile, and therefore should be given highest priority in federal programs.

Develop a National Road Map with a Specific Timetable for Ending Petroleum Imports

PCAP proposes that we cut America's oil consumption in half by 2020, without additional domestic production of conventional oil, and without substituting alternative fuels that complicate the climate problem. The President should create a National Commission on Energy and Climate Security consisting of government and private experts, and charge it with creating a "road map" to the 2020 goal and beyond. The road map should include not only clean fuels and more efficient vehicles, but also mass transit, high-speed rail, transit-oriented development, and other strategies to reduce vehicle miles 20 percent by 2020 and 50 percent by 2050.

Reduce the Vulnerability of the Nation's Energy Infrastructure

In a videotape released in December 2005, al Qaeda leader Ayman al-Zawahiri encouraged his followers to attack America's energy infrastructure. It's an easy target. It consists of more than 160,000 miles of crude oil pipelines, 4,000 offshore platforms, 10,400 power plants, 160,000 miles of transmission lines, gas transportation and storage facilities, and port terminals for liquefied natural gas. Much of it is virtually impossible to protect from sabotage.

The President should propose that Congress, the Department of Energy, state regulators, local utilities, and building designers make much greater use of distributed electric generation such as rooftop solar collectors and community-scale wind turbines, which depend less on transmission lines and are harder to disrupt. Further, the President can direct that all infrastructure projects involving federal funds must include materials and design features that "harden" the projects against natural disasters, terrorism, and the impacts of climate change. He should direct the U.S. Departments of Transportation and Energy to develop guidelines on designs and materials that will accomplish these goals.

Redefine National Security and Defense

The conclusion that climate change is a national security issue leads to an interesting thought: We may have come to a time when solar collectors and plug-in hybrid vehicles are as vital to national defense as M-16 rifles and tanks.

There are a number of things the Defense Department must do to prepare for climate change—for example, protecting coastal military installations from sea-level rise. But a vital task for national security will be defense-by-prevention—that is, working now to minimize the dangers of oil dependence and global warming. Judging by our investments, that's not our strategy now. In 2008, the government budgeted only $7.37 billion to slow climate change, while budgeting nearly $650 billion for military security. During the last five years, the ratio of military security to climate security spending has averaged ninety-seven to one.

The President should establish the policy that national defense and security require an end to America's dependence on oil and a dramatic reduction in U.S. greenhouse gas emissions. Under this model, defense investments will include decentralizing and hardening sensitive infrastructure, diversifying energy supplies, reducing the nation's dependence on vital and strategically important imported and finite resources, helping developing nations adopt climate-friendly technologies and resources, and collaborating with other countries on energy independence and greenhouse gas reductions.

We may find that this type of defense investment improves the economy. Researchers at the University of Massachusetts Amherst have concluded that $1 billion invested in personal consumption, health care, education, mass transit, home weatherization, and infrastructure all create more jobs than the same amount spent on the military.

The President should direct the National Security Council to recommend how we will reinvent national defense for the new realities of the twenty-first century. We shouldn't be preparing to fight the wars of the past; we should be preventing the wars of the future.

11.

Rejoining the International Community

The salvation of mankind lies only in making everything the concern of all.

—Aleksandr Solzhenitsyn

In 1980, a United Nations official made a prescient observation. The greatest danger in the years ahead, he said, is not the nuclear bomb. It's the "aspiration bomb"—the unfulfilled aspirations of billions of the world's people who would like to achieve a standard of living comparable to the one we enjoy in the United States.

But if developing nations take the same path to industrialization as we took—consuming enormous quantities of natural resources including fossil fuels—climate change will be catastrophic. The challenge is to help developing nations leap over our old path to find a new and better one.

Cell phones are a good example of leapfrog technology. If you visit parts of Asia that are developing rapidly, you're not likely to see telephone poles and lines. People have moved directly to wireless telecommunications. The same has to happen with how electricity is generated, cars are made, buildings are built, and factories are powered in emerging economies. They need to leap over resource-intensive designs and processes, and move directly into the low-carbon future.

The way to defuse the aspiration bomb is not to ask people to stop aspiring. The solution is to create and disseminate the tools people need to address what the United Nations calls the two defining challenges of the twenty-first century: climate change and poverty.

Let's be honest. The world community is justified to feel that the United States must be a big part of the climate solution, both in reducing our own emissions and in helping developing nations avoid them. We are the world's most powerful country, its richest people, its most innovative talent pool of scientists and engineers, and the nation most responsible for the greenhouse gas emissions concentrated in the atmosphere today.

But there are pragmatic as well as ethical and humanitarian reasons to help end global poverty with clean technologies. The jobs and investment data I cited in Chapter 2 give strong evidence that the global requirement for low-emission technologies and products is an enormous opportunity for new jobs, businesses, and progress here at home.

The past eight years have not been good for America's image overseas. The new presidency is an opportunity to start over. Whether we are motivated by altruism or by self-interest, we need to embark on that new beginning. No nation, not even the most powerful on earth, can tackle today's climate, energy, and security challenges alone. The following are some of the early steps the new President should take.

Send Immediate Signals of Commitment to Global Climate Leadership

Before inauguration, the President-elect should signal the United States' commitment to international collaboration on climate action. First, he should state that the climate challenge will be one of the central commitments of his administration. He should say that he is committed to setting ambitious targets for emission reductions in the United States and to the international goal of keeping global warming to no more than 2 degrees Celsius above preindustrial levels. Second, he should reaffirm the United States' intention to cooperate in the Bali Action Plan—the agreement reached in Bali, Indonesia, in December 2007 to negotiate a carbon-reduction agreement to succeed the Kyoto Protocol. By endorsing the Bali plan, the President-elect will embrace the goal that industrialized nations will reduce their greenhouse gas emissions 25–40 percent below 1990 levels by 2020. Third, the President-elect should send a high-level representative to attend the 14th Conference of the Parties, an international meeting scheduled for December 2008 in Poznan, Poland, where countries will begin drafting the post-Kyoto agreement that the international community hopes to approve a year later in Copenhagen. His emissary should interact informally with representatives of other nations to gather insights on the key issues and dynamics involved with climate negotiations.

Meet with Congress

After inauguration, the President and his key Cabinet members should meet early with congressional leaders to agree on principal elements of a national climate policy, including the steps the United States will take leading up to the Copenhagen meeting. A key question is the timing of congressional action on a cap-and-trade regime. On the one hand, passage of legislation would show the nation's commitment to climate action, giving the United States greater credibility in Copenhagen. On the other hand, there's a danger that any bill passed by Congress in 2009 would reduce U.S. negotiating flexibility in Copenhagen and would have to be redone later so that U.S. action is consistent with the international post-Kyoto agreement. Another issue is that the goal of reducing greenhouse gases 25–40 percent by 2020 is far more ambitious than any of the bills introduced so far in Congress. The President and congressional leaders should agree on how to show substantial movement on domestic climate policy before Copenhagen. This early meeting should be the beginning of an ongoing collaboration that builds trust and consensus between the executive and legislative branches to avoid gridlock in federal climate leadership.

Go to China

During 2009, the President or his representatives will attend a number of meetings with world leaders, including a G-8 summit in Maddalena, Italy. The President should make climate change— particularly the role of industrialized nations—a central topic of these meetings. In addition, the President should meet as early as possible in 2009 with President Hu Jintao of China to discuss the special responsibilities of the world's two largest emitters of greenhouse gases. The President should propose and seek approval early in 2009 of a bilateral Executive Agreement on Joint Climate Action with China—a pact with both substantive and symbolic importance in demonstrating collaboration between developed and developing nations.*

---

* China already has committed to significant action. It has set a goal of reducing the energy intensity of its economy 20 percent by 2010, has established vehicle efficiency standards higher than those in the United States, and plans to obtain 15 percent of

Review the Priorities of the Asia-Pacific Partnership

In 2005, the Bush administration announced the creation of the Asia-Pacific Partnership on Clean Development and Climate, a seven-nation collaboration to accelerate the development and commercialization of low-carbon energy technologies. Members include Canada, China, India, Japan, South Korea, Australia, and the United States, collectively responsible for more than 50 percent of the world's energy use and greenhouse gas emissions. The President should direct the Secretary of Energy to review the objectives and work of the partnership to make sure that it reflects the administration's goal to reduce international reliance on fossil energy imports.

Improve the Environmental Performance of World Development Assistance

Much of the United States' international development effort is carried out through the World Bank, the Overseas Private Investment Corp., the Export-Import Bank, and sister institutions. Part of the mission of these banks has been to create fossil energy sectors in developing nations to satisfy the growing energy needs of industrialized nations. The President should champion reforms to decarbonize the development programs and focus them on renewable energy projects in the developing world.

The President should advocate, too, that international development programs improve their performance on meeting other important environmental objectives. A July 2008 report by the

---

its energy from renewable resources by 2020. It's estimated that voluntary emission reductions already underway in China, Brazil, and Mexico alone are greater than those achieved by the countries that signed the Kyoto Protocol.

Independent Evaluation Group, based on an examination of $400 billion in investments in nearly seven thousand projects, concluded that environmental and sustainability objectives often were not put into practice in projects financed by the World Bank and its sister institutions.

Propose the Creation of an International Renewable Energy Agency (IREA)

This agency would be funded by redirecting global subsidies that have traditionally supported carbon-intensive projects in the fossil and nuclear energy industries to renewable energy investments. The IREA would provide technical assistance through a worldwide network of experts in energy efficiency and renewable technology. Financing would be administered through an IREA Clean Energy Bank to provide micro-loans and grants as well as to facilitate technology transfer from the United States and other industrialized nations to the developing world.

Assess the Impact of Greenhouse Gas Emissions in the Developing World

There is no credible system in place to assess the full impact of greenhouse gas emissions in the developing world. The sources of emissions range from wood and dung fires, to methane from rice paddies, to deforestation. The administration should propose that such an assessment be done by the United Nations Environment Programme (UNEP) and should distinguish between "survival" and "luxury" emissions—in other words, carbon emissions from activities vital to providing basic needs versus those that are not.

Champion Clean Energy Sovereignty

Some of the important policies the United States and other nations can institute to fight global warming—for example, requirements that a percentage of their energy come from renewable resources—can be challenged as unfair trade practices under the current rules of the World Trade Organization (WTO). Climate protection should trump trade protection. Governments must have the authority to protect climate-friendly products from unfair imports, to institute domestic regulations designed to cut carbon, and to subsidize clean energy technologies without interference from trading rules. The President should advocate that national policies necessary to reduce greenhouse gas emissions should be exempted from WTO challenges.

Seek an International "Grand Deal" on Carbon Subsidies

A recent analysis by UNEP estimates that worldwide subsidies of fossil fuels may amount to as much as $300 billion annually. UNEP says that no truly reliable numbers are available on worldwide energy subsidies, given the size and complexity of the task. Estimates are that Russia has the largest subsidies, about $40 billion yearly, followed by $37 billion in Iran, and subsidies in excess of $10 billion each in China, Saudi Arabia, India, Indonesia, Ukraine, and Egypt.* Once the United States has begun an orderly phase-out of its fossil energy subsidies, the President should seek agreement among all nations to:

----

* As reported earlier, fossil energy subsidies in the United States also amount to tens of billions of dollars a year, but estimates vary widely depending on how they are defined and reported. When state and local subsidies are counted, the U.S. total is even higher.

- Inventory, quantify, and improve reporting of fossil energy subsidies
- Phase out the subsidies, preferably with funds redirected to energy efficiency and renewable energy technologies
- Facilitate the transfer of clean technologies and resources to the developing world to reduce their need for fossil fuels
- Establish an enforcement mechanism

EPILOGUE

On January 24, 2008, a few days before President George W. Bush was to deliver his final State of the Union address, the Presidential Climate Action Project sent a courier to the White House to deliver a document. We called it the "State of the Climate Message," and it carried the signatures of many of the nation's most prominent scientists and policy experts, as well as five recipients of the Nobel Peace Prize.

Our intention was to demonstrate that the state of the climate and the state of the union are inextricably linked. The latter utterly depends on the former. So, as the 44th President of the United States prepares to deliver his inaugural address and his first State of the Union address, we hope he will consider our message. We hope you'll join us in urging him to, because ultimately the President's willingness and power to address difficult issues comes from us—not from special interests, or Congress, or even the Constitution. Our votes are his mandate; our ideas are his inspiration; our support is his courage.

Here are some key excerpts from the State of the Climate Message:

As the United States approaches the end of the first decade of the twenty-first century, the most dangerous and difficult challenge of our time remains largely unaddressed. Global climate change continues unabated. The United States is the nation that is most responsible for the problem and most capable of contributing to the solution. Yet today, the United States stands virtually alone among developed nations in refusing to accept the need for decisive action.

Consequently, we regret to report that the state of the nation's climate policy is poor, and the climate and the ecosystems that depend upon it are showing increasing signs of disruption. Global climate change now threatens not only the environment, but also our national security, our economic stability, and our public health and safety. We can no longer discuss the state of the union without assessing the state of the nation's climate.

The growing consequences of climate change have not appeared without warning. . . . After twenty years of assessing evidence in the most thorough scientific undertaking in history, the Intergovernmental Panel on Climate Change (IPCC) has concluded unequivocally that climate change is underway, that it is primarily the result of our consumption of fossil fuels, and that time is growing short if we are to avoid catastrophic consequences on a global scale. As United Nations Secretary General Ban Ki-moon and the chair of the IPCC, Rajendra Pachauri, both have said, this is our defining moment.

Our nation has the ideas and many of the tools necessary to create a highly efficient economy powered by low-carbon, renewable, domestic resources, and is able to provide this and future generations with security, opportunity, and stewardship. We are ready for comprehensive, prompt, and transformative climate action. These positive developments are overwhelmed, however, by the growth in greenhouse gas emissions. Our emissions in the United States are among the highest in the world, roughly twice the per capita emissions of Western Europe or Japan. Yet the people of Western Europe and Japan outscore the people of the United States on several key quality-of-life indicators, including life expectancy and infant mortality.

Several critical developments must take place by the time the 44th President delivers the State of the Union address:

1. We must recognize that global climate change is an issue that transcends politics and partisanship. No responsible leader of any political persuasion wants our nation to face a future of increasing heat waves, drought, fires, disease, natural disasters, coastal inundation, and species extinction. No responsible leader wishes to bequeath to our children a nation in peril, with far less security, fewer resources, and a lower standard of living than we enjoy today.

2. We must accept that while climate science is complex, our options are simple. We have three. We can reduce greenhouse gas emissions to keep the impacts of climate change from growing far worse. We can adapt to the changes already underway. Or we can suffer. Some suffering is inevitable and we must help those least able to cope. But the more quickly we reduce emissions today and prepare for the consequences of emissions from the past, the less suffering there will be. Those are the realities that we must acknowledge and act upon now.

3. We must recognize that national climate policy and national energy policy are inextricably linked. The United

States must make a deliberate and rapid transition away from carbon-based fuels whose emissions cannot be captured and stored, whether the fuels come from foreign or domestic sources. We must turn with unprecedented speed to a future of energy independence, resource efficiency, renewable energy technologies, and low-carbon fuels. Public policy must support only those technologies and resources that simultaneously stabilize the climate and enhance national energy security.

4. We must acknowledge that global climate change is more than an environmental issue. It affects national security by threatening instability in some of the most volatile regions of the world. It is an urgent economic issue in which the price of action is much less than the cost of inaction. It is a public health issue in which the spread of diseases in a warmer world can have devastating implications for our well-being and the costs of health care. It is a humanitarian issue, with the prospect of hundreds of millions of people being displaced by drought, hunger, and coastal flooding. It is a population and quality of life issue, challenging us to find ways for the world's people to achieve and sustain a decent standard of living. It is a moral issue, testing our character and our sense of responsibility to those least able to cope with climate change, as well as to future generations.

5. We must recognize not only the existence and threat of climate change, but the enormous opportunities that we can capture by addressing it. The transformation to a clean economy can open paths of possibility to all Americans, including those the old economy left behind. As the world's leading innovator, we should become the

world's leading source of the technologies and products that will help all people in all nations—including our own—achieve dignity, security, and high quality of life, while dramatically reducing effects on climate.

6. In addition to reducing greenhouse gas emissions, we must protect the Earth's natural ecological systems, particularly forests, which are the lungs of the planet and play a critical role in sequestering greenhouse gases. We have a global obligation to protect the world's tropical forests and to restore those that have been degraded.

7. We must not wait for other nations to go first. Developed and developing nations both must hold greenhouse gas emissions in check. But the United States will have little influence on other nations until we lead by example with a credible, comprehensive domestic program. Our first step in constructive engagement with the international community must be concrete action at home.

8. We must break the grip of special interests that are working to perpetuate the technologies, resources, and practices that served us well in the past, but that now threaten our future. Special interests cannot be allowed to prevail over the public good. We must vastly increase support for research, development, and deployment of clean energy technologies, and encourage the coal, oil, and gas industries to invest in these technologies for their future, as well as the nation's.

9. We must restore federal funding for Earth sciences and expand our research into the regional, local, social, and economic impacts of climate change. The national Climate Change Science Program must produce the

knowledge and deliver the information the American people need to mitigate, anticipate, and adapt to the adverse impacts of global warming. We must engage the talents of our best scientists and engineers and restore respect for science in the federal government.

10. We must redefine "clean" and think long-term. Each product and energy resource must be evaluated for climate impact over its entire life cycle. A fuel that emits little carbon when it generates energy, but that produces significant greenhouse gas emissions when it is mined, refined, and transported, is not truly clean. A biofuel that reduces oil imports but destroys our soils is not sustainable.

11. Finally, we must recognize that global climate change is the leadership issue of our time. Given the long lag time involved in reducing atmospheric concentrations of carbon, we cannot procrastinate any longer. This is indeed the defining moment for each of us as voters and consumers, for our generation, for our leaders, and for our world. We must not fail.

It is our hope and expectation that when the next President of the United States reports on the state of the union, we will hear that our nation is firmly on the path to climate stability, to a new economy that has learned to prosper within the limits of the Earth's natural systems, to energy independence and security, and to renewed respect for the United States around the world.

Can the next President save the planet in 100 days? Of course not. Even the world's most powerful leader can't do this job alone. It will take all nations and many years of sustained effort. But in those first few months of his administration, the President can and must rally his administration, the Congress, and the American people to set to work together, before it's too late.

If this is our defining moment, then let us be known as a people of courage, morality, vision, and goodwill—a people who gladly accept the responsibility of ensuring that the America of tomorrow is even better than the America of today. That commitment to the future is required of us if we wish to keep faith with those who founded our nation, with those who have sacrificed for it, and with those around the world who look to the United States of America for hope.

APPENDIX A

What You Can Do

The climate problem cannot be solved if the world's only super-power, the planet's biggest per capita energy user, and the earth's richest nation sits on the sidelines. But in the final analysis, it will be individuals like you and me who solve the climate crisis.

The greenhouse gases we put in the atmosphere are the result of billions and billions of decisions individuals make every minute of every day. Do I turn off the light? Do I turn down the thermostat? Is my car due for a tune-up? Do I need to drive so fast, or so often? Should I take the bus today? Should I recycle that plastic bag from the grocery store or, better yet, bring my own? Should I use my tax refund, or my salary bonus, or my economic stimulus check to weatherize my house, to change all my lightbulbs to compact fluorescents, to buy an Energy Star appliance? Can I make my next car a hybrid? Should I take my retirement money out of companies that build coal plants and put it into green investments? And how do I use my vote?

At first, the climate crisis may seem too big to be solved by individual people. But it's a mistake to think you have no power to make a difference. Ideas for taking action are proliferating as individual Americans are creating blogs, organizing demonstrations, and working to elect the political candidates who have the commitment, the courage, and the sense of urgency to help us get the job done.

If you're interested in learning more about climate action, and if you're interested in doing more, here are some resources.

Get Inspired

Across the United States and around the world, the green shoots of a brand-new sustainable economy are beginning to appear. I've cited some of them in this book. If you'd like more examples of the impressive innovations underway in our country and case studies of how individuals have seized the initiative, check out *Apollo's Fire*, the wonderful book by U.S. Representative Jay Inslee and Bracken Hendricks of the Center for American Progress.

Get Knowledgeable

While the science of climate and the geopolitics of energy are complex, we are blessed with some very articulate scientists and observers who are helping us make sense of it all. Al Gore's book (and movie), *An Inconvenient Truth*, remains one of the best primers on the climate problem. If you'd like a vicarious journey to the places on the planet where climate change is most visible, read *Field Notes from a Catastrophe: Man, Nature and Climate Change*, by Elizabeth Kolbert. If you'd like to drill down into the oil issue, read *Freedom from Oil: How the Next President Can End the United States' Oil Addiction* by David Sandalow.

There are many excellent Web sites that can help you better understand and track developments in climate action. Here are ten of the most popular:

RealClimate: Climate science from climate scientists
Climate Progress: An insider's view of climate science, politics, and solutions

DeSmogBlog: Clears the public relations pollution that clouds climate science

Celsias: Cooling the planet one project at a time

It's Getting Hot In Here: Dispatches from the youth climate movement

Climate of Our Future: A discussion of climate change

Climate Ark: Climate change and global warming portal

SolveClimate.com: Daily climate news and opinion

A Few Things Ill Considered: A layman's take on the science of global warming featuring a guide on how to talk to a climate skeptic

Climate Feedback: An informal forum for debate and commentary on climate science

Get Busy

There are scores of checklists available that suggest what you can do to become a climate activist in your own home or business. Try these:

- The Web site of the National Leadership Summits for a Sustainable America features a personal action plan that I put together as part of a two-year effort to develop an action agenda to improve the nation's sustainability.

- The Alliance to Save Energy provides all you need to know about Job Number One, cutting your carbon emissions by improving your energy efficiency. The alliance's site has tips for consumers, educators, energy companies, and policy makers.

- The Climate Trust is a nonprofit organization that helps you calculate your carbon footprint—the carbon you're emitting in your home and business, and from your vehicle and air travel. Its Web site walks you through the calculations and shows you how to make contributions the trust invests in clean energy projects. (There are a growing number of carbon offset groups similar to the trust, but check them out before you buy an offset. Look for third-party certification of offset projects, a clear accounting of how your money will be spent, and what percentage of your donation will go to a clean energy project rather than to administrative overhead.)

- The We Campaign, a project of the Alliance for Climate Protection—the nonprofit effort founded by Al Gore—offers a commonsense agenda for personal action to cut carbon.

Get Involved

Elected leaders at every level need our help. To take the bold and sometimes politically risky action necessary to reinvent government for a postcarbon era, the President of the United States, your representatives in Congress, your governor and mayor, need a public mandate. They need to know that their constituents are behind them. In fact, they need to know that their political careers are at risk if they *don't* take bold action. If you'd like to be part of the marches, canvassing, and teach-ins of the electronic age, check out these organizations:

- The coalition 1Sky unites environmental, labor, faith-based, youth, and other organizations committed to speaking with one voice about climate action, and building a national network to get out the vote for climate change. The excellent list of 1Sky's allies will lead you to youth, faith, business, local government, civic, labor, and environmental organizations leading the climate-action movement.

- The We Campaign's goal is to build a movement that creates the political will to solve the climate crisis. Over 1.5 million people have already signed up.

- Stop Global Warming is a "virtual march" organized by Laurie David, who produced *An Inconvenient Truth*. More than 1 million Americans have signed up.

- The group known as 350 is an international effort launched by environmental author Bill McKibben and others to push for the United Nations and the United States to adopt the goal of reducing atmospheric carbon concentrations to 350 parts per million (from its current 385)—an ambitious target, but one NASA scientist Jim Hansen says is necessary to avert climate disaster.

- The Energy Action Coalition is an organization designed to help young Americans get active to help stop climate change.

These resources are just a sample of what's available today. There is no lack of opportunity to become a climate activist—and no excuse for remaining on the sidelines. It's time to light some candles.

APPENDIX B

The Use of Executive Authority

The new President will have to grapple with many perverse legacies of the Bush administration, among them a mistrust of what many critics see as an abuse of presidential power. A number of President Bush's actions—among them his order directing warrantless domestic surveillance and his use of signing statements as a virtual line-item veto of Congressional intent—led to protests that the President acted "contrary to the rule of law and our constitutional system of separation of powers," in the words of the American Bar Association.

The Bush legacy could lead Congress, the courts, the voters, and the opponents of climate action to push the presidential power pendulum to the opposite extreme—a very conservative interpretation of presidential authority that handcuffs the executive branch even in those areas where its powers are clear. From the standpoint of climate action, a handcuffed president would be a huge handicap. Congress is not built for speed and speed is what's required if we're to have a chance to mitigate climate change before it tips beyond our control. Indeed, while President Bush has been harshly criticized for avoiding significant action to fight climate change, Congress must share the blame. Under both Republican and Democratic control,

Congress has failed to establish carbon caps, a carbon price, or a coherent national energy policy.

The President's powers are conferred by the Constitution and by Congress. Congress makes the laws; the administration administers them. But Congress often delegates power to the President or to other administration officials to make key decisions on how laws are implemented. To avoid time-consuming controversy over the legitimate use of presidential power, the Presidential Climate Action Project commissioned the Center for Energy and Environmental Security (CEES) at the University of Colorado School of Law to analyze both the boundaries of executive authority and the affirmative responsibilities the law places on the executive branch in regard to environment, climate, and energy.

Looking to history as well as to the law, the authors of that report found a valuable model in President Franklin D. Roosevelt. Publicly, Roosevelt emphasized that it was his duty to serve the interests of the American people and he would not allow Congress to stand in the way. "In the event that Congress should fail to act, and act adequately, I shall accept the responsibility and I will act," he told Congress in his Labor Day address of 1942.

But in fact, he did not need to step over an inactive Congress. FDR was a popular president who entered office in the middle of the Great Depression and who, during his second term, was confronted with World War II. In those times of national emergency, the need for and popular support of strong leadership became clear. Roosevelt asked Congress to give him the new authorities he felt he needed to deal with the Depression, and Congress did so. On occasion, where he felt the need was urgent, FDR acted first and asked for Congress's blessing later, but his consultation with lawmakers and strong public demand for leadership avoided a power struggle—a struggle in which Congress has superior firepower.

Today, climate change is every bit as urgent a danger as a depression or war but in a different way. The effects we are beginning to experience now—glacial melting, sea-level rise, and extreme weather events, for example—are the result of greenhouse gas emissions from thirty, forty, or fifty years ago. The impact of greenhouse gases we are emitting today will be felt by our children and grandchildren. It is as though we are firing bullets today that will travel inexorably through time, their course unalterable, to strike the heart of the American Dream decades from now. The full consequence is distant but the cause immediate. The solution is to stop firing the bullets.

In addition to the authority current law gives the executive branch to act against climate change, the 44th President should ask that Congress grant the executive branch the latitude to respond rapidly to unanticipated climate impacts, in the same way past presidents have asked Congress for the authority to go to war, if national security warrants it.

As FDR put it, "It may be that an unprecedented demand and need for undelayed action may call for temporary departure from that normal balance of public procedure . . . and in the event that the national emergency is still critical, I shall not evade the clear course of duty that will then confront me. I shall ask the Congress for the one remaining instrument to meet the crisis—broad Executive power to wage a war against the emergency, as great as the power that would be given to me if we were in fact invaded by a foreign foe."

As CEES notes, "One of the key actions to be taken by a future President to address climate change policy would be to work with Congress for the appropriate and necessary delegations of authority that will give him or her the power to act with flexibility, without delay, and with certainty within the framework of the Constitution."

In addition to his existing powers and those additional powers he might request from Congress, the third indispensable element of presidential leadership is strong public support—a mandate, in fact, for decisive action from Washington. That is the course that offers the surest footing for national climate policy. As University of Chicago Professor William Howell has noted, "Not once in the modern era have the courts overturned a president who enjoys broad-based support from Congress, interest groups, and the public."

And that's the rub. Will "interest groups and the public" grasp how serious climate change is and how urgently the nation needs to move to a clean energy economy? Will we demand that our leaders finally act boldly, aggressively, and together? Our elected leaders, the scientific community, and all the organizations working to build grassroots awareness of the clear and present danger of climate change have an enormous responsibility now. We must build a public mandate that is stronger than economic inertia, stronger than the oil and coal lobbies, stronger than the arguments of the deniers, and stronger than our fear of change. Members of Congress must know that inaction, not action, is the surest way to lose their seats. The American people must know that the cost of doing nothing about climate change and energy security is far, far higher than the cost of intelligent action, and those costs will be assessed against the livelihoods, the health, and the safety of our children.

So, part of the President's challenge is not only to use his executive powers; he must also use his persuasive powers and his bully pulpit. As an example of how potent that power can be, the 44th President can turn to the 35th, John F. Kennedy, when he called forth the best of the American people to deal with the challenges of his time:

Today, every inhabitant of this planet must contemplate the day when this planet may no longer be habitable. Man holds in his mortal hands the power to abolish all forms of human poverty, and all forms of human life. We would like to live as we once lived, but history will not permit it.

Let us not seek the Republican answer or the Democratic answer; but the right answer. Let us not seek to fix the blame for the past. Let us accept our own responsibility for the future. I believe we possess all the resources and talents necessary. But the facts of the matter are that we have never made the national decisions or marshaled the national resources required for such leadership.

I look forward to a great future for America—a future in which our country will match its military strength with our moral restraint, its wealth with our wisdom, its power with our purpose. For time and the world do not stand still. Change is the law of life. And those who look only to the past or the present are certain to miss the future.

All this will not be finished in the first 100 days. Nor will it be finished in the first 1,000 days, nor in the life of this administration, nor perhaps in our lifetimes on this planet. But let us begin. Do not pray for easy lives. Pray to be stronger men.*

---

* This is a compilation of direct quotes from several different speeches by President Kennedy.

ACKNOWLEDGMENTS

This book is drawn from a much larger body of work prepared by the Presidential Climate Action Project over two years. Four individuals deserve special thanks for their intellectual and monetary support. Professor David Orr of Oberlin College not only thought of the idea for a hundred-day presidential action plan, but helped us find the funding to get started. Adam Lewis has been an extraordinarily generous principal sponsor, as he has been for so many initiatives on sustainable development and the environment. Ray Anderson, the captain of one of the world's greenest companies and the co-chairman of the President's Council on Sustainable Development, has presided over PCAP's National Advisory Committee, attending every minute of every meeting—a remarkable commitment from so busy a leader. U.S. Senator Gary Hart (ret.) has been an invaluable coach, drawing not only on his national security expertise and his gift as one of America's most thoughtful policy leaders, but also on his experience as a two-time candidate for the presidency. Thanks, too, to Dean Kathleen Beatty for her generous and steady support for the project at the University of Colorado.

The other members of the PCAP Advisory Committee have given the PCAP team their best guidance and, just as important, a license to be bold. When we began meeting early in 2007, the members of the committee agreed that consensus, often the enemy of boldness, would not be required on this project. Instead, they directed us to push the envelope of energy and climate policy. In addition to the people already mentioned, our distinguished advisors are Dr. D. James Baker, director of the Global Carbon Measurement Program at the William J. Clinton Foundation; Scott Bernstein, president of the Center for Neighborhood Technology; April Bucksbaum, executive director of the Baum Foundation; Brian Castelli, executive vice president of the Alliance to Save Energy; Dianne Dillon-Ridgley, chair of Plains Justice; Boyd Gibbons, past president of the Johnson Foundation; Sheila Slocum Hollis, partner, Duane Morris LLP; Van Jones, president of the board and co-founder of the Ella Baker Center for Human Rights; William C. Kunkler III, executive vice president of CC Industries Inc.; L. Hunter Lovins, president of Natural Capitalism Solutions Inc.; Michael Northrop, program director for sustainable development at the Rockefeller Brothers Fund; John L. Petersen, president of the Arlington Institute; Theodore Roosevelt IV, chair of the Pew Center on Global Climate Change; Larry Schweiger, president and CEO of the National Wildlife Federation (NWF); James Gustave Speth, dean of the Yale School of Forestry and Environmental Studies; Jeremy Symons, Global Warming Campaign director at NWF; Terry Tamminen, Cullman Senior Fellow and Climate Policy Director, New America Foundation; Vice Admiral Richard H. Truly, U.S. Navy Ret., former administrator of the National Aeronautics and Space Administration and former director of the National Renewable Energy Laboratory; and Heidi VanGenderen, former senior policy advisor on climate to Colorado Governor Bill Ritter.

Our many other financial sponsors have provided the resources for PCAP to commission studies, convene meetings, run a vibrant

Web site, conduct national opinion polls, build tools, publish results, and reach out to the community of organizations working on energy and climate issues. They include the Rockefeller Brothers Fund, the Rockefeller Family Fund, the Interface Environmental Fund, the Crown and Kunkler Family, the Sidney E. Frank Foundation, Tom and Noel Congdon, the Arntz Family Foundation, the Krehbiel Family Foundation, John and Laurie McBride, the Bermingham Fund, Susan Sakmar, Rutt Bridges, and Tara Trask. The Baum Foundation, the Johnson Foundation, Natural Capitalism Solutions Inc., and the University of Colorado Denver School of Public Affairs have provided in-kind support.

Literally hundreds of America's experts in energy, climate, the economy, business, and the environment have contributed to and/or reviewed this book. They are too numerous to name, but they know who they are. They gave their time and energy on faith that this project will make a difference.

I want to thank Barney Karpfinger for his role in bringing this book to production, and Bruce Shenitz for his invaluable help boiling down a large body of ideas into a size and form that I hope is digestible.

The other members of the PCAP team—Laurette Reiff, Diane Carman, and Morgan Pitts—have carried a tremendous workload in a very demanding enterprise these past two years. It has been a privilege to work with each of them.

WITHDRAWN

North Arkansas College
1515 Pioneer Drive
Harrison, AR 72601